1000 Years of Poetry

First published in 2000 by
Marino Books
An imprint of Mercier Press
16 Hume Street Dublin 2
Tel: (01) 661 5299; Fax: (01) 661 8583;
e.mail: books@marino.ie

Trade enquiries to CMD Distribution
55A Spruce Avenue
Stillorgan Industrial Park Blackrock
County Dublin
Tel: (01) 294 2556; Fax: (01) 294 2564
e-mail: cmd@columba.ie

© Introduction and Biographical Notes
Sean McMahon 2000
ISBN 1 86023114 4
10 9 8 7 6 5 4 3 2 1

A CIP record for this title is available
from the British Library
Cover design by SPACE
Printed by ColourBooks, Baldoyle
Industrial Estate, Dublin 13

1000 Years of Poetry A o'Halloran Dec 1998

A Millennial Anthology

Selected by Sean McMahon

Contents

Introduction

In Youth Is Pleasure

The Seasons' Difference

I Know My Love

Realms of Gold

The Humour o' It

The State of Man

Green and Pleasant Land

High Days and Holidays

Sunset and Evening Star

Biographical Index

Introduction

This is a personal but not, I hope, too idiosyncratic choice from the poetic treasure of the last one thousand years. Most of the entries are from the 'well of English undefiled', as Spenser in a different context described Chaucer, but there are also sprinklings of Latin and Irish since those traditions too are an essential part of our culture.

We all have a personal anthology in some recess of our brains, begun at parents' knees and added to at school, college and maturity. Memory being imperfect (though not for most of the poems we learnt in childhood) it is convenient to have a catholic selection in a form that we can risk handling roughly. This book is meant to lie at the bedside (or in the bathroom) and to hold some of the poems that we look for all of the time; there is no better lullaby than a sip from Helicon's stream.

The sharp-eyed will have noticed that all of the poets in this book joined the heavenly banquet some time before 1930, the year when according to EU prescription copyright begins. So such expected inclusions as Housman, Kipling, Chesterton, Frost and Yeats will not be found, but in spite of this grievous lack what remains is solid gold, tempered by the centuries and, national bristling aside, part of a common and matchless heritage.

Versions of Latin and Irish entries are by the compiler, except for the *Salve Regina* which has been in regular Church practice for hundred of years.

In Youth Is Pleasure

Gaudeamus

Anon (known 1267)

Universal student song still current in the early 20th century

Gaudeamus igitur,
Juvenes dum sumus.
Post jucundum juventutem,
Post molestam senectutem,
Nos habebit humus.

[Let us then rejoice, while we are young. After pleasant
   youth and irksome old age the earth shall claim us.]

In Youth Is Pleasure

Robert Wever (fl. 1550)

In a harbour grene aslepe whereas I lay,
The byrdes sang swete in the middes of the day,
I dreamed fast of mirth and play:
   In youth is pleasure, in youth is pleasure.

Methought I walked still to and fro,
And from her company I could not go –
But when I waked it was not so:
   In youth is pleasure, in youth is pleasure.

Therefore my heart is surely pyght
Of her alone to have a sight
Which is my joy and hartes delight:
   In youth is pleasure, in youth is pleasure.

Harbour = arbour; pyght = set

Golden Slumbers

Thomas Dekker (c. 1572–c. 1632)

Lullaby from the play *Patient Grissel* (1603)

Golden slumbers kiss your eyes,
Smiles awake you when you rise:
Sleep, pretty wantons, do not cry,
And I will sing a lullaby.
Rock them, rock them, lullaby.

Care is heavy, therefore sleep you.
You are care, and care must keep you:
Sleep, pretty wantons, do not cry,
And I will sing a lullaby.
Rock them, rock them, lullaby.

To the Virgins, to Make Much of Time

Robert Herrick (1591–1674)

Gather ye Rose-buds while ye may,
　　Old Time is still a-flying:
And this same flower that smiles today
　　Tomorrow will be dying

The glorious Lamp of Heaven, the Sun,
　　The higher he's a-getting
The sooner will his Race be run
　　And nearer he's to Setting.

That Age is best which is the first,
    When Youth and Blood are warmer
But being spent, the worse, and worst
    Times still succeed the former

Then be not coy, but use your time,
    And while ye may, go marry:
For having lost but once your prime,
    You may for ever tarry.

Beatha an Scoláire *[The student life]*

Anon (c. 1600 Century)

Aoibhinn beatha an scoláire
    bhíos ag déanamh a léighinn
is follas díbh, a dhaoine,
gurab dó is aoibhne in Éirinn.

Gan smacht ríogh ná rófhlatha
    ná tighearna dá threise
gan chuid cíosa ag caibidil
    gan moichéirge, gan meirse

Moichéirge ná aodhaireacht
    ní thabhair uadha choidhche,
's ní mó do-bheir dea aire
    fear na faire san oidhche

Do-bheir sé ar tháiplis,
    is ar chláirsigh go mbinne,
nó fós greas eile ar shuirghe
    is ar chumann mná finne.

Maith biseach a sheisrighe
  ag teacht tosaigh an earraigh;
is é crannghail dá sheisrigh
  lán a ghlaice de pheannaibh.

[The student's life is gear, man, poring through those books –
the best gaff in Ireland, as you folks well know.

No king or prince or any boss to shove you around; no fees
nor digs to pay for, no chores or early rising.

Lie till noon if you want; no gathering in the sheep or doing
security work at night.

Play chess, twang the harp, chase the bints.

When the spring comes, your team is in good nick; you
harrow with your pens.]

A Boy's Song

James Hogg (1770–1835)

Where the pools are bright and deep,
Where the grey trout lies asleep,
Up the river and over the lea,
That's the way for Billy and me.

Where the blackbird sings the latest,
Where the hawthorn blooms the sweetest,
Where the nestlings chirp and flee,
That's the way for Billy and me.

Where the mowers mow the cleanest,
Where the hay lies thick and greenest,
There to track the homeward bee,
That's the way for Billy and me.

Where the hazel bank is steepest,
Where the shadow falls the deepest,
Where the clustering nuts fall free,
That's the way for Billy and me.

Why the boys should drive away
Little sweet maidens from the play,
Or love to banter and fight so well,
That's the thing I never could tell.

But this I know, I love to play
Through the meadow, among the hay;
Up the water and over the lea,
That's the way for Billy and me.

[from] Lines composed a few miles above Tintern Abbey, on revisiting the banks of the Wye during a tour July 13, 1798

William Wordsworth (1770–1850)

For nature then
(The coarser pleasures of my boyish days,
And their glad animal movements all gone by)
To me was all in all – I cannot paint
What then I was. The sounding cataract
Haunted me like a passion; the tall rock,
The mountain, and the deep and gloomy wood,
Their colours and their forms, were then to me
An appetite, a feeling and a love
That had no need of a remoter charm,
By thought supplied, nor any interest
Unborrowed from the eye. – That time is past,
And all its aching joys are now no more,
And all its dizzy raptures. Not for this
Faint I, nor mourn nor murmur; other gifts

Have followed; for such loss, I would believe,
Abundant recompense. For I have learned
To look on nature, not as in the hour
Of thoughtless youth; but hearing oftentimes
The still, sad music of humanity,
Nor harsh nor grating, though of ample power
To chasten and subdue. And I have felt
A presence that disturbs me with the joy
Of elevated thoughts; a sense sublime
Of something far more deeply interfused,
Whose dwelling is the light of setting suns,
And the round ocean and the living air,
And the blue sky, and in the mind of man:
A motion and a spirit, that impels
All thinking things, all objects of all thought,
And rolls through all things. Therefore am I still
A lover of the meadows and the woods,
And mountains; and of all that we behold
From this green earth; of all the mighty world
Of eye, and ear, – both what they half create,
And what perceive; well pleased to recognise
In nature and the language of the sense
The anchor of my purest thoughts, the nurse,
The guide, the guardian of my heart, and soul
Of all my moral being.

A Visit from St Nicholas

Clement Clarke Moore (1779–1863)

Written in 1822 for the poet's own family this children's classic was
first printed on 23 December 1823 in the *Troy Sentinel* New York

'Twas the night before Christmas, when all through the
     house
Not a creature was stirring, not even a mouse;
The stockings were hung by the chimney with care,
In hopes that St Nicholas soon would be there;
The children were nestled all snug in their beds,
While visions of sugarplums danced in their heads:
And mamma in her 'kerchief, and I in my cap,
Had just settled down for a long winter's nap –
When out on the lawn there arose such a clatter,
I sprang from my bed to see what was the matter.
Away to the window I flew like a flash,
Tore open the shutters, and threw up the sash.
The moon on the breast of the new-fallen snow,
Gave the lustre of midday to objects below;
When, what to my wondering eyes should appear,
But a miniature sleigh and eight tiny reindeer,
With a little old driver, so lively and quick,
I knew in moment it must be St Nick.
More rapid than eagles his coursers they came,
And he whistled, and shouted, and called them by
     name:
'Now *Dasher*! now, *Dancer*! now, *Prancer* and *Vixen*!
On *Comet*! on, *Cupid*! on, *Donder* and *Blitzen*!
To the top of the porch! to the top of the wall!
Now dash away! dash away! dash away all!'
As dry leaves before the wild hurricane fly,
When they meet with an obstacle, mount to the sky;
So up to the house-top the coursers they flew

With the sleigh full of toys, and St Nicholas too.
And then, in a twinkling, I heard on the roof
The prancing and pawing of each little hoof –
As I drew in my head, and was turning around,
Down the chimney St Nicholas came with a bound.
He was dressed all in fur, from his head to his foot,
And his clothes were all tarnished with ashes and soot;
A bundle of toys he had flung on his back,
And he looked like a pedlar just opening his pack.
His eyes – how they twinkled: his dimples how merry!
His cheeks were like roses, his nose like a cherry!
His droll little mouth was drawn up like a bow,
And the beard of his chin was as white as the snow;
The stump of his pipe he held tight in his teeth,
And the smoke it encircled his head like a wreath;
He had a broad face and a little round belly
That shook, when he laughed, like a bowl full of jelly.
He was chubby and plump, a right jolly elf,
And I laughed when I saw him in spite of myself;
A wink of his eye and a twist of his head
Soon gave me to know I had nothing to dread;
He spoke not a word, but went straight to his work,
And filled all the stockings; then turned with a jerk,
And laying his finger aside of his nose,
And giving a nod, up the chimney he rose;
He sprang to his sleigh, to his team gave a whistle,
And away they all flew like the down of a thistle.
But I heard him exclaim, ere he drove out of sight,
'Happy Christmas to all, and to all a good night!'

Young and Old

Charles Kingsley (1819–75)

When all the world is young, lad
    And all the trees are green;
And every goose a swan, lad,
    And every lass a queen;
Then hey for boot and spur, lad,
    And round the world away;
Young blood must have its course, lad,
    And every dog its day.

When all the world is old, lad,
    And all the trees are brown;
And all the sport is stale, lad,
    And all the wheels run down;
Creep home and take your place there,
    The spent and maimed among:
God grant you find one face there,
    You loved when all was young.

Escape at Bedtime

Robert Louis Stevenson (1850–94)

The lights from the kitchen and parlour shone out
Through the blinds and the windows and bars;
And high overhead and all moving about
There were millions and millions of stars.

There ne'er were such thousands of leaves on a tree,
Nor of people in church or the park,
As the crowds of the stars that looked down upon me,
And glittered and winked in the dark.

The Dog and the Plough, and the Hunter, and all
And the star of the sailor, and Mars,
These shone in the sky, and the pail by the wall
Would be half full of water and stars.

They saw me at last, and they chased me with cries,
And soon had me back into bed;
But the glory kept shining and bright in my eyes,
And stars going round in my head.

the star of the sailor = Polaris

The Seasons' Difference

Sumer Is Icumen In

Anon (c. 1226)

Earliest extant English song lyric set as a *rota* or round for four tenors
and two basses by a monk of Reading Abbey

Sumer is icumen in,
Lhude sing cuccu!
Groweth sed and bloweth med
And springeth the wode nu
Sing cuccu!

Awe bleteth after lomb
Lhouth after calve cu
Bulluc sterteth, bucke verteth
Murie sing cuccu!

Cuccu, cuccu
Wel singes thu cuccu
Ne swike thu naver nu!

Sing cuccu nu. Sing cuccu!
Sing cuccu,
Sing cuccu nu!

med = meadow; awe = ewe; lhouth = lows; verteth = farts; murie =
merry; swik = cease

Anon (c. 1300)

Lenten ys come with love to toune,
With blosmen and with briddes roune,
   That al this blisse bryngeth;
Dayes-eyes in this dales,
Notes suete of nyhtegales,
   Uch foul song singeth;
The threstelcoc him treteth oo,
Away is huere wynter wo,
   When woderove springeth;
Thise foules singeth ferly fele,
Ant wlyeth on huere wunne wele,
   That al the wode ryngeth.

blosmen = blossom; briddes roune = birds' song; foul = full; him treteth
oo = keeps chattering; wo =woe; woderove = woodruff; foules = fowls;
ferly fele = many; Ant wlyeth on huere wunne wele = whistle for joy

[from] The Canterbury Tales; The Prologue

Geoffrey Chaucer (c. 1345–1400)

When that Aprille with his shoures sote
The droghte of March hath perced to the rote
And bathed every veyne in swich licour,
Of which vertu engendred is the flour;
When Zephirus eek with his swete breeth
Inspired hath in every holt and heeth
The tender croppes, and the yonge sonne
Hath in the Ram his halfe cours y-ronne,
And smale fowles maken melodye,
That slepen al the night with open yë,
(So priketh hem nature in hir corages):
Then longen folk to go on pilgrimages
(And palmers for to seken straunge strondes)
To ferne hawles, couthe in sondry londes;
And specially, from every shires ende
Of Engelond, to Caunterbury they wende,
The holy blisful martir for to seke,
That hem hath holpen, whan that they were seke.

sote = sweet; rote = root; Zephirus = west wind; Ram = Aries (21 March
– 20 April); so priketh hem nature in hir corages = such is the effect
of nature; ferne hawles = distant shrines; holy blisful martir = Thomas
à Becket (d. 1170); holpen = helped; seke = sick

Nicholas Breton (c. 1545–c. 1626)

In the merry month of May,
In a morn at break of day,
Forth I walked by the wood side,
Whereas May was in his pride.
There I spied all alone
Phyllida and Corydon.
Much ado there was, God wot,
He would love and she would not.
She said, never man was true;
He said, none was false to you.
He said, he had loved her long;
She said, love should have no wrong.
Corydon would kiss her then;
She said, maids must kiss no men,
Till they did for good and all.
Then she made the shepherd call
All the heavens to witness truth,
Never loved a truer youth.
Thus with many a pretty oath,
Yea and nay, and faith and troth,
Such as silly shepherds use,
When they will not love abuse,
Love, which had been long deluded,
Was with kisses concluded:
And Phyllida with garlands gay
Was made the Lady of the May.

Winter

Edmund Spenser (1552–99)

From *The Pageant of the Seasons and Months* (1595)

Lastly, came *Winter* clothed all in frize,
Chattering his teeth for cold that did him chill,
Whil'st on his hoary beard his breath did freeze
And the dull drops that from his purpled bill
As from a limbeck did adown distill.
In his right hand a tipped staff he held,
With which his feeble steps he stayed still:
For he was faint with cold, and weak with eld
That scarce his loosed limbes he able was to weld.

frize = frieze cloth; limbeck = retort; eld = age; weld = control

Whenas the Rye Reach to the Chin

George Peele (1558–1597)

Song from the play *The Old Wives' Tale* (1595)

Whenas the rye reach to the chin,
And chopcherry, chopcherry ripe within,
Strawberries swimming in the cream,
And schoolboys playing in the stream;
    Then O, then O, then O my true love said,
        Till that time come again,
    She could not live a maid.

Now Is the Month of Maying

Anon (16th Century)

Song lyric from a collection made by Thomas Morley, 1595

Now is the month of maying,
When merry lads are playing
Each with his bonny lass
Upon the greeny grass.

The spring, clad all in gladness,
Doth laugh at winter's sadness,
And to the bagpipe's sound
The nymphs tread out their ground.

Fie then! why sit we musing,
Youth's sweet delight refusing?
Say, dainty nymphs, and speak,
Shall we play barley-break?

barley-break = game of tig, played by three couples

Spring

William Shakespeare (1564-1616)

From *Love's Labour's Lost* (1594)

When daisies pied and violets blue
　　And lady-smocks all silver white
And cuckoo-buds of yellow hue
　　Do paint the meadows with delight,
The cuckoo then, on every tree
Mocks married men; for thus sings he
　　　　Cuckoo;
Cuckoo, cuckoo: Of word of fear,
Unpleasing to a married ear!

When shepherds pipe on oaten straws,
　　And merry larks are ploughmen's clocks,
When turtles tread, and rooks, and daws,
　　And maidens bleach their summer smocks
The cuckoo then, on every tree
Mocks married men; for thus sings he
　　　　Cuckoo;
Cuckoo, cuckoo: Of word of fear,
Unpleasing to a married ear!

turtles = doves

Autolycus' Song

William Shakespeare (1564–1616)

From *A Winter's Tale* (1611)

When daffodils begin to peer,
    With heigh! the doxy, over the dale,
Why, then comes the sweet o' the year;
    For the red blood reigns in the winter's pale.

The white sheet bleaching on the hedge,
    With heigh! the sweet birds, Oh how they sing!
Doth set my pugging teeth an edge,
    For a quart of ale is a dish for a king.

The lark, that tirra-lirra chants,
    With heigh! With heigh! the thrush and the jay,
Are summer songs for me and my aunts,
    While we lie tumbling in the hay.

pugging = stealing; aunts = loose wenches

William Shakespeare (1564-1616)

From *Love's Labour's Lost* (1594)

When icicles hang by the wall,
    And Dick the shepherd blows his nail,
And Tom bears logs into the hall,
    And milk comes frozen home in pail,
When blood is nipped and ways be foul
Then nightly sings the staring owl
        Tu-whit, to-who,
A merry note,
When greasy Joan doth keel the pot

When all aloud the wind doth blow,
    And coughing drowns the parson's saw
And birds sit brooding in the snow,
    And Marian's nose looks red and raw
When roasted crabs hiss in the bowl,
Then nightly sings the staring owl
        Tu-whit, to-who,
A merry note,
When greasy Joan doth keel the pot

keel = cool; saw = proverb; crabs = small apples

Spring

Thomas Nashe (1567–1601)

From the play *Summer's Last Will and Testament* (1593)

Spring, the sweet Spring, is the year's pleasant king;
Then blooms each thing, then maids dance in a ring,
Cold doth not sting, the pretty birds do sing, –
    Cuckoo, jug-jug, pu-we, to-witta-woo!

The palm and may make country houses gay,
Lambs frisk and play, the shepherds pipe all day,
And we hear aye birds tune this merry lay, –
    Cuckoo, jug-jug, pu-we, to-witta-woo!

The fields breathe sweet, the daisies kiss our feet,
Young lovers meet, old wives a-sunning sit,
In every street these tunes our ears do greet, –
    Cuckoo, jug-jug, pu-we, to-witta-woo!
       Spring! the sweet Spring.

may = hawthorn blossom

[as] Cill Aodáin *[from Killeden]*

Antaine Ó Reachtabhra (1784–1835)

Anois teacht an earraigh beidh an lá 'dul 'un síneadh
    's tar éis na Féile Bríde ardóidh mé mo sheol,
's ó chuir mé 'mo cheann é ní chónóidh mé choíche
    go seasfaidh mé thíos i lár Chontae Mhaigh Eo;

i gClár Chlainne Muiris a bheas mé an chéad oíche
  's i mBalla, taobh thíos de, 's ea thosós mé ag ól,
go Coillte Mach rachad go ndéanad cuairt mhíosa ann,
  i bhfoisceacht dhá mhíle do Bhéal an Átha Móir

Fágaim le uachta go n-éiríonn mo chroíse
  Mar ardaíos an ghaoth nó mar scaipeas an ceo
nuair a smaoiním ar Chearra nó ar Ghaileang taobh thíos de,
  ar Sceathach an dá Mhíle 's ar phlánaí Mhaigh Eo
Chill Aodáin, an bhaile a bhfásann gach ní ann;
  bíonn sméara 's sú craobh ann is meas ar gach sórt;
's dá mbeinnse 'mo sheasamh i gceartlár mo dhaoine
  d' éireodh an aois dhíom is bheinn arís óg.

[Now with the coming of spring, the days have a bit of a stretch
and after St Brigid's Day I'll hoist my sail. Since the idea struck
me I'll not wait a single night till I find myself there in the heart
of Mayo. I'll spend the first night in Claremorris and in Balla
beyond it I'll start on the booze. Then to Kiltimagh and I'll
spend a good month there and *it's* quite contagious to Ballinamore.

My hand on my heart but my spirits start to soar as the gale rises
or the fog drifts away when I think about Carra or Gaileang
beside it or Srathangaveela or Mayo's broad plains. Killeden's the
place where everything grows. It has blackberries, raspberries
and fruit of all sorts. If I were only there among my own people,
age would fall from me and I'd be young again.]

[from] Ode to the West Wind

Percy Bysshe Shelley (1792–1822)

I

O wild West Wind, thou breath of Autumn's being,
Thou from whose unseen presence the leaves dead
Are driven, like ghosts from an enchanter fleeing,

Yellow, and black, and pale, and hectic red,
Pestilence-stricken multitudes: O thou,
Who chariotest to their dark wintry bed

The wingèd seeds, where they lie cold and low,
Each like a corpse within its grave, until
Thine azure sister of the Spring shall blow

Her clarion o'er the weeping earth, and fill
(Driving sweet buds like flocks to feed on air)
With living hues and odours plain and hill.

Wild Spirit, which art moving everywhere;
Destroyer and preserver; hear oh, hear!

II

Thou on whose stream, mid the steep sky's commotion,
Loose clouds like earth's decaying leaves are shed,
Shook from the tangled boughs of Heaven and Ocean,

Angels of rain and lightning: there are spread
On the blue surface of thine airy surge,
Like the bright hair uplifted from the head

Of some fierce Maenad, even from the dim verge
Of the horizon to the zenith's height,
The locks of the approaching storm. Thou dirge

Of the dying year, to which this closing night
Will be the dome of a vast sepulchre,
Vaulted with all thy congregated might

Of vapours, from whose solid atmosphere
Black rain, and fire, and hail shall burst: oh, hear!

V

Make me thy lyre, even as the forest is:
What if my leaves are falling like its own!
The tumult of thy mighty harmonies

Will take from both a deep autumnal tone,
Sweet though in sadness. Be though, Spirit fierce,
My spirit! Be thou me impetuous one!

Drive my dead thoughts over the universe
Like withered leaves to quicken a new birth!
And, by the incantation of this verse,

Scatter as from an unextinguished hearth
Ashes and sparks, my words among mankind!
Be through my lips to unawakened earth

The trumpet of a prophecy! O, Wind,
If Winter comes, can Spring be far behind?

Ode to Autumn

John Keats (1795–1821)

Season of mists and mellow fruitfulness!
    Close bosom-friend of the maturing sun;
Conspiring with him how to load and bless
    With fruit the vines that round the thatch-eaves
        run;
To bend with apples the moss'd cottage-trees,
    And fill all fruit with ripeness to the core;
        To swell the gourd, and plump the hazel shells
    With a sweet kernel; to set budding more,
And still more, later flowers for the bees,
Until they think warm days will never cease,
        For Summer has o'er-brimmed their clammy
        cells.

Who hath not seen thee oft amid thy store?
    Sometimes whoever seeks abroad may find
Thee sitting careless on a granary floor,
    Thy hair soft-lifted by the winnowing wind;
Or on a half-reap'd furrow sound asleep,
    Drowsed with the fumes of poppies, while thy hook
        Spares the next swath and all its twinèd flowers;
And sometimes like a gleaner thou dost keep
    Steady thy laden head across a brook;
    Or by a cider-press, with patient look,
        Thou watchest the last oozings, hours by hours.

Where are the songs of Spring? Ay, where are they?
    Think not of them, thou hast thy music too,
        While barrèd clouds bloom the soft-dying day,
And touch the stubble-plains with rosy hue.
    Then in a wailful choir the small gnats mourn
    Among the river shallows, borne aloft

Or sinking as the light wind lives and dies;
And full-grown lambs bleat from hilly bourn;
   Hedge-crickets sing; and now with treble soft
The redbreast whistles from a garden-croft,
    And gathering swallows twitter in the sky.

Thugamar Féin an Samradh Linn
[We've brought summer with us]

Anon (18th Century)

Thugamar féin an samradh linn!
Thugamar féin an samradh linn!
Thugamar linn é, 's cé bhainfeadh dínn é!
'S thugamar féin an samradh linn!

Samradh! Samradh! bainne na ngamhna!
Thugamar féin an samradh linn.
Samradh buí ó luí na gréine!
Thugamar féin an samradh linn.
   Cuileann is coll is trom is caorthainn,
   Thugamar féin an samradh linn.
   Is fuinseog ghléigeal bhéil an átha,
   Thugamar féin an samradh linn.

'Sé seo an samhradh thiocfas go haerach
Thugamar féin an samradh linn.
Samhradh buí na nóinín gléigeal,
Thugamar féin an samradh linn.
   Thugamar linn é ón gcoill chraobhaigh,
   Thugamar féin an samradh linn.
   Ó bhaile go baile 's go dtí n-ár tigh féinig,
   Thugamar féin an samradh linn.

Do bheatha, mo dheartháir, is fada nach bhfaca é!
Thugamar féin an samradh linn.
Nó mo bhean phósta, ós í is giorra dhom!
Thugamar féin an samradh linn.
   Suíodh sí síos ar chathaoir airgid
   Thugamar féin an samradh linn.
   Nó ar chathaoir órga, más í sin is fearr léi!
   Thugamar féin an samradh linn.

Babóg na Bealtaine, maighdean an tsamhraidh,
Thugamar féin an samradh linn.
Cailíní maiseacha bán-gheala gléasta
'S thugamar féin an samradh linn.
   Samradh! Samradh! bainne an ngamhna!
   Thugamar féin an samradh linn;
   Samradh! Samradh! bainne an ngamhna!
   Thugamar féin an samradh linn.

[We've brought summer with us!
We've brought it with us; who'll take it from us?
We've brought summer with us!

Summer, summer, rich with calves' milk;
We've brought summer with us!
Summer still golden after sunset.
We've brought summer with us!
Holly and hazel, elder and rowan;
We've brought summer with us!
White-blossomed ash at the mouth of the fording;
We've brought summer with us!

This is the summer that's coming so gaily;
We've brought summer with us!
The golden summer filled with bright daisies;
We've brought summer with us!
We've brought it with us from the branchy wood;
We've brought summer with us!

From village to village and then into our houses;
We've brought summer with us!

Greetings, my brother, it's long since we saw it!
We've brought summer with us!
And my own wife since she's closer still
We've brought summer with us!
Let her be seated on a chair of silver;
We've brought summer with us!
Or on one of gold if that's what she wants!
We've brought summer with us!

Queen of the May, maiden of summer!
We've brought summer with us!
Beautiful colleens all dressed in white
We've brought summer with us!
Summer, summer, rich with calves' milk;
We've brought summer with us!
Summer, summer, rich with calves' milk;
We've brought summer with us!]

Autumn

Henry Wadsworth Longfellow (1807–82)

Thou comest, Autumn, heralded by rain,
 With banners, by great gales incessant fann'd,
 Brighter than brightest silks of Samarkand,
 And stately oxen harness'd to thy wain;
Thou standest, like imperial Charlemagne,
 Upon thy bridge of gold; thy royal hand
 Outstretch'd with benedictions o'er the land,
 Blessing the farms through all thy vast domain.
Thy shield is the red harvest moon, suspended
 So long beneath the heaven's o'erhanging eaves;
Thy steps are by the farmer's prayers attended;
 Like flames upon an altar shine the sheaves;
And, following thee, in thy ovation splendid,
 Thine almoner, the wind scatters the golden leaves!

The Darkling Thrush

Thomas Hardy (1840–1928)

I leant upon a coppice gate
 When Frost was spectre-gray,
And Winter's dregs made desolate
 The weakening eye of day.
The tangled bine-stems scored the sky
 Like strings of broken lyres,
And all mankind that haunted nigh
 Had sought their household fires.

The land's sharp features seemed to be
    The Century's corpse outleant,
His crypt the cloudy canopy,
    The wind his death-lament.
The ancient pulse of germ and birth
    Was shrunken hard and dry,
And every spirit upon earth
    Seemed fervourless as I.

At once a voice arose among
    The bleak twigs overheard
In a full-hearted evensong
    Of joy illimited;
An aged thrush, frail, gaunt, and small,
    In blast-beruffled plume,
Has chosen thus to fling his soul
    Upon the growing gloom.

So little cause for carolings
    Of such ecstatic sound
Was written on terrestrial things
    Afar or nigh around,
That I could think there trembled through
    His happy goodnight air
Some blessed Hope, whereof he knew
    And I was unaware.

I Know My Love

De Ramis Cadunt Folia
[The Leaves Fall from the Branches]

Anon (c. 1200)

De ramis cadunt folia
    nam vigor totus periit
iam calor liquit omnia
    at abiit;
nam signa coeli ultima
    sol petiit.

Iam nocet frigus teneris
    et avis bruma leditur
et philomena ceteris
    conqueritur,
quod illis ignis etheris
    adimitur.

Nec lympha caret alveus,
    nec prata virent herbida,
sol nostra fugit aureus
    confinia;
est inde dies niveus,
    nox frigida.

Modo frigescit quidquid est,
    sed solus ego caleo;
immo sic mihi cordi est
    quod ardeo;
hic ignis tamen virgo est,
    qua langueo.

Nutritur ignis osculo
  et leni tactu virginis;
in suo lucet oculo
  lux luminis,
nec est in toto seculo
  plus numinis.

Ignis grecus extinguitur
  cum vino iam acerrimo;
sed iste non extinguitur
  miserrimo:
immo fomento alitur
  uberrimo.

[The leaves fall from the branches for all strength has gone; now the warmth has left and the sun heads into the last stellar house.

Frost attacks the young plants and the birds feel the winter's cold. The nightingale complains to her kind that the fire of heaven is dimmed.

The streams are swollen and the meadows are no longer green. The golden sun has left our regions; the days are snowfilled, nights arctic.

All around me freezes; I alone am burning. There is a fire in my heart, the girl for whose love I am weak.

The fire is fuelled by the kiss and gentle touch of this girl. In her eye gleams the light of lights; there is nothing in the whole world so divine.

Greek fire can be quenched by vinegar but bitter wine rather nourishes mine. Even that bitterness is sweet.]

Praise of Women

Robert Mannyng of Brunne (1288–1338)

Interpolation into his *Handlyng Synne* (1303) by a Gilbertine monk of Bourne in Lincolnshire

No thyng is to man so dere
As wommanys love in gode manere.
A gode womman is mannys blys,
There here love right and steadfast is.
There is no solas under hevene
Of alle that a man may nevene,
That shuld a man do so moche glew
As a gode womman that loveth trew.
Ne derer is none in Goddys hurde
Than a chaste womman with lovely worde.

nevene = name; glew = gladness; hurde = herd

Walsingham

Sir Walter Raleigh (c. 1552–1618)

In Norfolk, it became the major English Marian shrine in 1601

'As you came from the holy land
   Of Walsingham,
Met you not with my true love
   By the way as you came?'

'How shall I know your true love,
   That have met many a one
As I went to the holy land,
   That have come, that have gone.'

'She is neither white nor brown
    But as the heavens fair,
There is none hath a form so divine
    In the earth or air.'

'Such a one did I meet, good Sir,
    Such an angelic face,
Who like a queen, like a nymph did appear
    By her gait, by her grace.'

'She hath left me here all alone,
    All alone as unknown,
Who sometimes did me lead with herself,
    And me loved as her own.'

'What's the cause that she leaves you alone
    And a new way doth take,
Who loved you once as her own
    And her joy did you make?'

'I loved her all my youth,
    But now old, as you see,
Love likes not the falling fruit
    From the withered tree.

'Know that Love is a careless child,
    And forgets promise past;
He is blind, he is deaf when he list
    And in faith never fast.

'Her desire is a dureless content
    And a trustless joy;
He is won with a world of despair
    And is lost with a toy.

'Of womenkind such indeed is the love
   Of the word love abused,
Under which many childish desires
   And conceits are excused.

'But true Love is a durable fire
   In the mind ever burning;
Never sick, never old, never dead,
   From itself never turning.'

dureless = not lasting

Love's Farewell

Michael Drayton (1563–1631)

Since there's no help, come let us kiss and part, –
Nay I have done, you get no more of me;
And I am glad, yea, glad with all my heart,
That thus so cleanly I myself can free
Shake hand for ever, cancel all our vows,
And when we meet at any time again,
Be it not seen in either of our brows
That we one jot of former love retain.
Now at the last gasp of Love's latest breath,
When his pulse failing, Passion speechless lies,
When Faith is kneeling by his bed of death,
And innocence is closing up his eyes,
– Now if thou woulds't, when all have given him over
From death to life thou mightst him yet recover!

Shall I Compare Thee . . .

William Shakespeare (1564–1616)

Sonnet XVIII

Shall I compare thee to a summer's day?
Thou art more lovely and more temperate:
Rough winds do shake the darling buds of May,
And summer's lease hath all too short a date.
Sometime too hot the eye of heaven shines
And often is his gold complexion dimmed;
And every fair from fair sometime declines,
By chance or nature's changing course untrimmed.
But thy eternal summer shall not fade,
Nor lose possession of that fair thou ow'st,
Nor shall Death brag thou wand'rest in his shade,
When in eternal lines to time thou grow'st.
    So long as men can breathe or eyes can see,
    So long lives this, and this gives to thee.

My Mistress' Eyes . . .

William Shakespeare (1564–1616)

Sonnet CXXX

My mistress' eyes are nothing like the sun;
Coral is far more red than her lips' red;
If snow be white, why then her breasts are dun;
If hairs be wires, black wires grow on her head.
I have seen roses damask'd, red and white,
But no such roses see I in her cheeks;
And in some perfumes is there more delight
Than in the breath that from my mistress reeks.

I love to hear her speak, yet well I know
That music hath a far more pleasing sound;
I grant I never saw a goddess go;
My mistress, when she walks, treads on the ground:
    And yet, by heaven, I think my love as rare
    As any she belied with false compare.

To Celia

Ben Jonson (1573–1637)

A versification of the prose of the fourth-century Greek writer
Philostratus, published in 1616

Drink to me only with thine eyes,
    And I will pledge with mine;
Or leave a kiss but in the cup
    And I'll not look for wine.
The thirst that from the soul doth rise
    Doth ask a drink divine;
But might I of Jove's nectar sip
    I would not change for thine.

I sent thee late a rosy wreath
    Not so much honouring thee
As giving it a hope that there
    It could not wither'd be
But thou thereon didst only breathe
    And sens't it back to me;
Since then it grows and smells, I swear,
    Not of itself but thee.

John Donne (1572–1631)

Licence my roving hands, and let them go,
Before, behind, between, above, below.
O my America!, my new-found-land,
My kingdom, safeliest when with one man man'd,
My mine of precious stones, My Emperie,
How blest I am in this discovering thee!
To enter in these bonds, is to be free;
Then where my hand is set, my seal shall be.
    Full nakedness! All joys are due to thee,
As souls unbodied, bodies unclothed must be,
To taste whole joys. Gems which you women use
Are like Atlanta's balls, cast in men's views,
That when a fool's eye lighteth on a gem,
His earthly soul may covet theirs, not them.
Like pictures, or like books gay covering made
For laymen, are all women thus array'd;
Themselves are mystick books, which only we
(Whom their imputed grace must dignify)
Must see reveal'd. Then since that I may know;
As liberally as to a midwife, shew
Thy self: cast all, yea, this white linen hence,
Here is no penance, much less innocence.
    To teach thee I am naked first; why then
What needst thou have more covering than a man.

There Is a Lady Sweet and Kind

Anon (16th Century)

There is a lady sweet and kind,
Was never face so pleased my mind;
I did but see her passing by,
And yet I love her till I die.

Her gesture, motion, and her smiles,
Her wit, her voice, my heart beguiles,
Beguiles my heart, I know not why,
And yet I love her till I die.

Her free behaviour, winning looks,
Would make a lawyer burn his books;
I touched her not, alas, not I,
And yet I will love her till I die.

Had I her fast betwixt mine arms
Judge you that think such sports are harms,
Were it any harm? No, no, fie fie!
For I will love her till I die.

Should I remain confinèd there
So long as Phoebus in his sphere,
I to request, she to deny,
Yet would I love her till I die.

Cupid is wingèd and doth range,
Her country so my love doth change;
Yet change she earth or change she sky,
Yet will I love her till I die.

Robert Herrick (1591–1674)

Her eyes the glow-worm lend thee,
The shooting stars attend thee,
  And the little elves also,
  Whose little eyes glow,
Like sparks of fire befriend thee.

No will-o'-th'-wisp mis-light thee;
Nor snake, or slow-worm bite thee;
  But on, on thy way
  Not making a stay,
Since ghost there's none to fright thee.

Let not the dark thee cumber;
What though the moon does slumber?
  The stars of the night
  Will lend thee their light,
Like tapers clear without number.

Then Julia let me woo thee,
Thus, thus to come unto me:
  And when I shall meet
  Thy silv'ry feet,
My soul I'll pour into thee.

Go, Lovely Rose

Edmund Waller (1606–87)

Written in 1645 while in banishment for treason against Parliament

Go lovely Rose!
Tell her that wastes her time and me,
That now she knows,
When I resemble her to thee,
How sweet and fair she seems to be.

Tell her that's young
And shuns to have her graces spied,
That hadst thou sprung
In deserts where no men abide,
Thou must have uncommended died

Small is the worth
Of beauty from the light retired:
Bid her come forth
Suffer herself to be desired
And not blush so to be admired.

Then die – that she
The common fate of all things rare
May read in thee:
How small a part of time they share
That are so wondrous sweet and fair!

Richard Crashaw (1613–49)

Whoe'er she be
That not impossible she
That shall command my heart and me;
....
I wish her beauty
That owes not its duty
To gaudy tire, or glistring shoe-tie

Something more than
Taffeta or tissue can,
Or rampant feather, or rich fan.

More than the spoil
Of shop, or silkworm's toil
Or a bought blush, or a set smile.

A face that's best
By its own beauty drest,
And can alone command the rest.

A face made up
Out of no other shop
Than nature's white hand set ope.

A cheek where youth,
And blood, with pen of truth
Write, what the reader sweetly ru'th

A cheek where grows
More than a morning rose:
Which to no box his being owes.

Lips, where all day
A lover's kiss may play,
Yet carry nothing thence away.

To Lucasta, Going to the Wars

Richard Lovelace (1618–58)

Tell me not, Sweet, I am unkind,
    That from the nunnery
Of thy chaste breast, and quiet mind,
    To war and arms I fly.

True: a new mistress now I chase
    The first foe in the field;
And with a stronger faith embrace
    A sword, a horse, a shield

Yet this inconstancy is such
    As thou too shalt adore;
I could not love thee dear so much
    Loved I not honour more.

To His Coy Mistress

Andrew Marvell (1621–1678)

Had we but world enough, and time,
This coyness, Lady, were no crime.
We should sit down and think which way
To walk and pass our long love's day.
Thou by the Indian Ganges' side
Shouldst rubies find: I by the tide

Of Humber would complain. I would
Love you ten years before the Flood,
And you should, if you please, refuse
Till the conversion of the Jews.
My vegetable love should grow
Vaster than empires but more slow;
An hundred years should go to praise
Thine eyes and on thy forehead gaze;
Two hundred to adore each breast;
But thirty thousand to the rest;
An age at least to every part,
And the last age should show thy heart;
For, Lady, you deserve this state
Nor would I love at lower rate.

   But at my back I always hear
Time's wingèd chariot hurrying near
And yonder all before us lie
Deserts of vast eternity.
Thy beauty shall no more be found
Nor, in thy marble vault, shall sound
My echoing song: then worms shall try
That long preserved virginity,
And your quaint honour turn to dust
And into ashes all my lust:
The grave's a fine and private place,
But none, I think, do there embrace.

   Now therefore, while the youthful hue
Sits on thy skin like morning dew,
And while the willing soul transpires
At every pore with instant fires,
Now let us sport us while we may,
And now, like amorous birds of prey,
Rather at once our time devour
Than languish in his slow-chapt power.
Let us roll all our strength and all
Our sweetness up into one ball,
And tear our pleasures with rough strife

Through the iron gates of life:
Thus, though we cannot make our sun
Stand still, yet we will make him run.

A Song of a Young Lady to Her Ancient Lover

John Wilmot, Earl of Rochester (1647–80)

Ancient person, for whom I
All the flattering youth defy,
Long be it ere thou grow old,
Aching, shaking, crazy, cold,
But still continue as thou art,
Ancient person of my heart.

On thy withered lips and dry,
Which like barren furrows lie,
Brooding kisses I will pour
Shall thy youthful heart restore;
Such kind showers in Autumn fall
And a second spring recall
Nor from thee will ever part
Ancient person of my heart.

Thy nobler part, which but to name
In our sex would be counted shame,
By age's frozen grasp possessed,
From its ice shall be released,
And, soothed by my reviving hand,
In former warmth and vigour stand.
All a lover's wish can reach
For thy joy my love shall reach,
And for thy pleasure shall improve
All that art can add to love.
Yet still I love thee without art
Ancient person of my heart.

'Where-e'er You Walk'

Alexander Pope (1688–1744)

From *Pastorals:* 'Summer', written when the poet was sixteen

Where-e'er you walk, cool gales shall fan the glade,
Trees, where you sit, shall crowd into a shade,
Where-e'er you tread, the blushing flow'rs shall rise,
And all things flourish where you turn your eyes.
Oh! how I long with you to pass my days,
Invoke the Muses, and resound your praise;
Your praise the birds shall chant in ev'ry grove
And winds shall waft it to the pow'rs above.
And wou'd you sing and rival Orpheus' strain,
The wond'ring forests soon should dance again,
The moving mountains hear the pow'rful call,
And headlong streams hang list'ning in their fall!
　　But see, the shepherds shun the noon-day heat,
The lowing herds to murm'ring brooks retreat,
To closer shades the panting flocks remove,
Ye Gods! and is there no relief for love?
But soon the sun with milder rays descends
To the cool ocean, where his journey ends;
On me love's fiercer flames for ever prey,
By night he scorches, as he burns by day.

A Red, Red Rose

Robert Burns (1759–96)

Burns's most famous love song, printed in 1793

O, my Luve's like a red, red rose,
　　That's newly sprung in June:
O my Luve's like a melodie
　　That's sweetly play'd in tune.

As fair art thou, my bonie lass,
　　So deep in luve am I:
And I will luve thee still, my Dear,
　　Till a' the seas gang dry.

Till a' the seas gang dry, my dear,
　　And the rocks melt wi' the sun:
And I will luve thee still, my Dear,
　　While the sands o' life shall run.

And fare thee weel, my only Luve,
　　And fare thee weel a while!
And I will come again, my Luve,
　　Tho' it ware ten thousand mile!

My Bony Mary

Robert Burns (1759–96)

Go, fetch to me a pint o' wine,
    And fill it in a silver tassie;
That I may drink before I go
    A service to my bonnie lassie.
The boat rocks at the Pier o' Leith,
    Fu' loud the wind blaws frae the Ferry,
The ship rides by the Berwick-law,
    And I maun leave my bony Mary.

The trumpets sound, the banners fly,
    The glittering spears are ranked ready,
The shouts o' war are heard afar,
    The battle closes deep and bloody:
It's not the roar o' sea or shore,
    Wad mak me langer wish to tarry:
Nor shouts o' war that's heard afar,
    It's leaving thee, my bony Mary!

The Lass of Richmond Hill

Leonard McNally (1757–1820)

Song written by one of the most successful Crown 'moles' to infiltrate
the United Irishmen. The lass was a Miss Anson from Yorkshire and
she became the poet's wife.

On Richmond Hill there lives a lass,
More bright than Mayday morn,
Whose charms all other maids surpass,
A rose without a thorn.

This lass so neat, with smiles so sweet,
Has won my right goodwill.
I'd crowns resign to call thee mine,
Sweet lass of Richmond Hill;
Sweet lass of Richmond Hill,
Sweet lass of Richmond Hill,
I'd crowns resign to call thee mine,
Sweet lass of Richmond Hill.

Ye zephyrs gay that fan the air,
And wanton thro' the grove,
O whisper to my charming fair,
'I die for her I love.'
This lass so neat, with smiles so sweet,
Has won my right goodwill.
I'd crowns resign to call thee mine,
Sweet lass of Richmond Hill;
Sweet lass of Richmond Hill,
Sweet lass of Richmond Hill,
I'd crowns resign to call thee mine,
Sweet lass of Richmond Hill.

Rose Aylmer

Walter Savage Landor (1775–1864)

Ah what avails the sceptred race!
    Ah what the form divine!
What every virtue, every grace!
    Rose Aylmer, all were thine.
Rose Aylmer, whom these wakeful eyes
    May weep but never see,
A night of memories and of sighs
    I consecrate to thee.

I Know Where I'm Going

Anon (19th century)

I know where I'm going,
I know who's going with me,
I know who I love,
But the dear knows who I'll marry.

I'll have stockings of silk
Shoes of fine green leather,
Combs to buckle my hair
And a ring for every finger.

Feather beds are soft,
Painted rooms are bonny;
But I'd leave them all
To go with my loved Johnny

Some say he's black,
I say he's bonny,
He's the flower of them all
My handsome coaxing Johnny.

I know where I'm going,
I know who's going with me,
I know who I love,
But the dear knows who I'll marry.

The Ways of Love

Elizabeth Barrett Browning (1806–1861)

One of the *Sonnets from the Portuguese* (1850), ostensibly translations, but really addressed to Robert Browning who called her 'the Portuguese' as a pet name.

How do I love thee? Let me count the ways.
I love thee to the depth and breadth and height
My soul can reach, when feeling out of sight
For the ends of Being and ideal Grace.
I love thee to the level of every day's
Most quiet need, by sun, by candlelight.
I love thee freely, as men strive for Right:
I love thee purely, as they turn from Praise.
I love thee with the passion put to use
In my old griefs, and with my childhood's faith.
I love thee with a love I seemed to lose
With my lost saints, – I love thee with the breath,
Smiles, tears, of all my life! – and, if God choose
I shall but love thee better after death.

The Lost Mistress (1845)

Robert Browning (1812–1889)

All's over then: does truth sound bitter
    As one at first believes?
Hark, 'tis the sparrows' goodnight twitter
    About your cottage eaves!

And the leaf-buds on the vine are woolly,
    I noticed that, today;
One day more burst them open fully
    – You know the red turns grey.

Tomorrow we meet the same, then, dearest?
    May I take your hand in mine?
Mere friends are we, – well, friends the merest
    Keep much that I resign:

For each glance of the eye so bright and black,
    Though I keep with heart's endeavour, –
Your voice, when you wish the snowdrops back,
    Though it stay in my soul for ever! –

Yet I will but say what mere friends say,
    Or only a thought stronger;
I will hold your hand but as long as all may,
    Or so very little longer!

Romance

Robert Louis Stevenson (1850–94)

I will make you brooches and toys for your delight
Of birdsong at morning and star-shine at night.
I will make a palace fit for you and me
Of green days in forest and blue days at sea.

I will make my kitchen and you shall keep your room
Where white flows the river and bright blows the
      broom,
And you shall wash your linen and keep your body
      white
In rainfall at morning and dewfall at night.

And this shall be for music when no one else is near,
The fine song for singing, the rare song to hear!
That only I remember, that only you admire,
Of the broad road that stretches and the roadside fire.

Arab Love Song

Francis Thompson (1859–1907)

The hunchéd camels of the night
Trouble the bright
And silver waters of the moon.
The Maiden of the Morn will soon
Through Heaven stray and sing,
Star gathering.

Now while the dark about our loves is strewn
Light of my dark, blood of my heart, O come!
And Night will catch her breath up, and be dumb.

Leave thy father, leave thy mother
And thy brother;
Leave the black tents of thy tribe apart!
Am I not thy father and thy brother,
And thy mother?
And thou – what needest thou with thy tribe's black
        tents
Who hast the red pavilions of my heart?

The 'hunchéd camels' are a well-known cloud formation in the desert.

Non Sum Qualis Eram Bonae sub Regno Cynarae
[I am not as I was when the good Cynara was my queen]

Ernest Dowson (1867–1900)

The title comes from the first poem in Horace's *Odes IV* (23BC)

Last night, ah, yesternight, betwixt her lips and mine
There fell thy shadow, Cynara! thy breath was shed
Upon my soul between the kisses and the wine;
And I was desolate and sick of an old passion
    Yea, I was desolate and bowed my head:
I have been faithful to thee, Cynara! in my fashion.

All night upon mine heart I felt her warm heart beat,
Night-long within mine arms in love and sleep she lay;
Surely the kisses of her bought red mouth were sweet;
But I was desolate and sick of an old passion,
    When I awoke and found the dawn was gray:
I have been faithful to thee, Cynara! in my fashion.

I have forgot much, Cynara! gone with the wind,
Flung roses, roses riotously with the throng,
Dancing, to put thy pale, lost lilies out of mind:
But I was desolate and sick of an old passion,
    Yea all the time because the dance was long:
I have been faithful to thee, Cynara! in my fashion.

I cried for madder music and for stronger wine
But when the feast is finished and the lamps expire,
Then falls thy shadow, Cynara! the night is thine;
And I was desolate and sick of an old passion,
    Yea, hungry for the lips of my desire:
I have been faithful to thee, Cynara! in my fashion.

Realms of Gold

'Imagination'

William Shakespeare (1564–1616)

From *A Midsummer Night's Dream* (1596)

The lunatic, the lover and the poet,
Are of imagination all compact;
One sees more devils than vast hell can hold,
That is, the madman; the lover, all as frantic,
Sees Helen's beauty in a brow of Egypt:
The poet's eye, in a fine frenzy rolling,
Doth glance from heaven to earth, from earth to
      heaven:
And as imagination bodies forth
The forms of things unknown, the poet's pen
Turns them to shapes, and gives to airy nothing
A local habitation and a name.

'Rough Magic'

William Shakespeare (1564–1616)

From *The Tempest* (1612)

             I have bedimmed
The noontide sun, called forth the mutinous winds,
And 'twixt the green sea and the azured vault
Set roaring war; to the dread rattling thunder
Have I given fire, and rifted Jove's stout oak
With his own bolt; the strong-based promontory
Have I made shake, and by the spurs plucked up
The pine and cedar; graves at my command
Have waked their sleepers, oped, and let 'em forth

By my so potent art. But this rough magic
I here abjure, and when I have required
Some heavenly music – which even now I do –
To work mine end upon their senses that
This airy charm is for, I'll break my staff,
Bury it certain fathoms in the earth,
And deeper than did ever plummet sound
I'll drown my book.

The Reaper

William Wordsworth (1770–1850)

Behold her, single in the field,
   Yon solitary Highland Lass!
Reaping and singing by herself;
   Stop here, or gently pass!
Alone she cuts and binds the grain,
And sings a melancholy strain;
O listen! for the vale profound
Is overflowing with the sound.

No nightingale did ever chaunt
   More welcome notes to weary bands
Of travellers in some shady haunt,
   Among Arabian sands:
A voice so thrilling ne'er was heard
In springtime from the cuckoo bird,
Breaking the silence of the seas
Among the farthest Hebrides.

Will no one tell me what she sings?
    Perhaps the plaintive numbers flow
For old, unhappy, far-off things
    And battles long ago:
Or is it some more humble lay,
Familiar matter of today?
Some natural sorrow, loss or pain
That has been and may be again?

Whate'er the theme, the maiden sang
    As if her song could have no ending;
I saw her singing at her work,
    And o'er her sickle bending;
I listen'd, motionless and still;
And, as I mounted up the hill,
The music in my heart I bore,
Long after it was heard no more.

Kubla Khan

Samuel Taylor Coleridge (1772–1834)

Poem written in 1797 in Somerset and generated partly by laudanum, which Coleridge took for his chronic toothache, and partly by his reading of the travels of Marco Polo in Asia. The lines recalled after a sleep were written down immediately on awaking but 'a person from Porlock' interrupted the flow and the rest was never recovered.

In Xanadu did Kubla Khan
A stately pleasure dome decree;
Where Alph, the sacred river, ran
Through caverns measureless to man
    Down to a sunless sea.
So twice five miles of fertile ground
With walls and towers were girdled round:

And there were gardens bright with sinuous rills
Where blossomed many an incense-bearing tree;
And here were forest ancient as the hills
Enfolding sunny spots of greenery.

But O, that deep romantic chasm which slanted
Down the green hill athwart a cedarn cover!
A savage place! as holy and enchanted
As e'er beneath a waning moon was haunted
By woman wailing for her demon-lover!
And from this chasm, with ceaseless turmoil seething,
As if this earth in fast thick pants were breathing,
A mighty fountain momently was forced;
Amid whose swift half-intermitted burst
Huge fragments vaulted like rebounding hail,
Or chaffy grain beneath the thresher's flail:
And 'mid these dancing rocks at once and ever
It flung up momently the sacred river.
Five miles meandering with a mazy motion
Through wood and dale the sacred river ran,
Then reached the caverns measureless to man,
And sank in tumult to a lifeless ocean:
Amid this tumult Kubla heard from far
Ancestral voices prophesying war!

The shadow of the dome of pleasure
        Floated midway on the waves;
Where was heard the mingled measure
        From the fountain and the caves
    It was a miracle of rare device,
    A sunny pleasure-dome with caves of ice!

A damsel with a dulcimer
        In a vision once I saw:
It was an Abyssinian maid,
        And on her dulcimer she play'd
Singing of Mount Abora.

Could I revive within me,
    Her symphony and song,
To such a deep delight 'twould win me,
That with music loud and long,
I would build that dome in air,
That sunny dome! those caves of ice!
And all who heard should see them there,
And all should cry, Beware! Beware!
His flashing eyes, his floating hair!
Weave a circle round him thrice,
    And close your eyes with holy dread,
    For he on honeydew hath fed,
And drunk the milk of paradise.

On First Looking into Chapman's Homer

John Keats (1795–1821)

The verse translations of Homer's *Iliad* and *Odyssey* were completed by
George Chapman (*c.* 1560–1634) in 1614.

Oft have I travell'd in the realms of gold,
    And many goodly states and kingdoms seen;
    Round many western islands have I been
Which bards in fealty to Apollo hold.
Oft of one wide expanse had I been told
    That wide-brow'd Homer ruled as his demesne;
    Yet never did I breathe its pure serene
Till I heard Chapman speak out loud and bold:
Then felt I like some watcher of the skies
    When a new planet swims into his ken;
Or like stout Cortez when with eagle eyes
    He stared at the Pacific – and all his men
Look'd at each other with a wild surmise –
    Silent, upon a peak in Darien.

[from] The Rubá'iyát of Omar Khayyám of Naishápur

Edward Fitzgerald (1809–1893)

Fitzgerald's version of the quatrains (*rubais*) of the Persian poet, astronomer and mathematician, Omar the Tentmaker (d.1123) was wildly popular with the late Victorians, many of whom were unaware that his beloved was a boy.

I

Awake! for Morning in the bowl of Night
Has flung the stone that puts the Stars to Flight:
   And Lo! the Hunter of the East has caught
The Sultan's Turret in a Noose of Light.

VII

Come, fill the cup, and in the Fire of Spring
The Winter garment of Repentance fling:
   The Bird of Time has but a little way
To fly – and Lo! the Bird is on the Wing.

XI

Here with a Loaf of Bread beneath the Bough
A Flask of Wine, a book of Verse – Thou
   Beside me singing in the Wilderness
And Wilderness is Paradise enow.

XVI

Think, in this battered Caravanserai
Whose Doorways are alternate Night and Day,
   How Sultán after Sultán with his Pomp
Abode his Hour or two, and went his way.

XVIII

I sometimes think that never blows so red
The Rose as where some buried Caesar bled;
    That every Hyacinth the Garden wears
Drops in his Lap from some once lovely head.

XXVI

Myself when young did eagerly frequent
Doctor and Saint, and heard great Argument
    About it and about; but evermore
Came out by the same Door as in I went.

XLIX

'Tis all a Chequer-board of Nights and Days
Where Destiny with Men for Pieces plays:
    Hither and thither moves, and mates, and slays,
And one by one back in the Closet lays.

LI

The Moving Finger writes; and having writ,
Moves on: nor all the Piety nor Wit
    Shall lure it back to cancel half a line
Nor all thy Tears wash out a Word of it.

LXXIV

Ah, Moon of my Delight who knows no wane,
The Moon of Heaven is rising once again:
    How oft hereafter rising shall she look
Though this same Garden after me – in vain!

To Helen

Edgar Allan Poe (1809–49)

Helen, thy beauty is to me
   Like those Nicéan barks of yore
That gently, o'er a perfumed sea,
   The weary way-worn wanderer bore
   To his native shore.

On desperate seas long wont to roam,
   Thy hyacinth hair, thy classic face,
Thy Naiad airs have brought me home
   To the glory that was Greece,
   And the grandeur that was Rome.

Lo! in yon brilliant window niche
   How statue-like I see thee stand,
   The agate lamp within thy hand!
Ah, Psyche, from the regions which
   Are Holy Land!

Now Sleeps the Crimson Petal

Alfred Lord Tennyson (1809–92)

Now sleeps the crimson petal, now the white;
Now waves the cypress in the palace walk;
Now winks the gold fin in the porphyry font
The firefly wakens: waken thou with me.

Now droops the milk-white peacock
And like a ghost she glimmers on to me
Now lies the earth all Danaë to the stars
And all thy heart lies open unto me.

Now slides the silent meteor on, and leaves
A shining furrow, as thy thoughts in me.

Now folds the lily all her sweetness up,
And slips into the bosom of the lake;
So fold thyself, my dearest, thou, and slip
Into my bosom and be lost in me.

The Splendour Falls

Alfred Lord Tennyson (1809-92)

Poem suggested by a trip to Killarney; the castle was Muckross Abbey
and the blowing of the bugle a regular tourist attraction.

The splendour falls on castle walls
    And snowy summits old in story:
The long light shakes along the lakes,
    And the wild cataract leaps in glory.
Blow, bugle, blow, set the wild echoes flying,
Blow, bugle; answer echoes, dying, dying, dying.

O hark!, O hark! how thin and clear,
    And thinner, clearer, farther going!
O sweet and far from cliff and scar
    The horns of Elfland faintly blowing!
Blow, let us hear the purple glens replying:
Blow, bugle; answer echoes, dying, dying, dying.

O love, they die in yon rich sky,
    They faint on hill or field or river:
Our echoes roll from soul to soul,
    And grow for ever and for ever.
Blow, bugle, blow, set the wild echoes flying,
And answer, echoes, answer, dying, dying, dying.

Frater, Ave atque Vale

Alfred Lord Tennyson (1809–92)

Tennyson's tribute to fellow poet Gaius Valerius Catullus (*c.* 84–*c.* 54
BC) who wrote a poem in praise of his 'paene insula Sirmio' in Lake
Garda. The bits of Latin are from the original poem.

Row us out from Desenzano, to your Sirmione row!
So they rowed, and there we landed – 'O venusta
      Sirmio!'
There to me through all the groves of olive in the
      summer glow,
Came the 'Ave atque Vale' of the Poet's hopeless woe,
Tenderest of Roman poets, nineteen-hundred years ago,
'Frater Ave atque Vale' – as we wandered to and fro
Gazing at the Lydian laughter of the Garda lake below
Sweet Catullus's all-but-island, olive silvery Sirmio!

Frater, Ave atque Vale = Hail and farewell, brother; *O venusta Sirmio*
= Lovely Sirmione!

The Fairies

William Allingham (1824–89)

Written at Halloween in Killybegs when the poet was twenty-five

Up the airy mountain,
    Down the rushy glen,
We daren't go a-hunting
    For fear of little men;
Wee folk, good folk,
    Trooping all together;
Green jacket, red cap,
    And white owl's feather!

Down along the rocky shore
    Some make their home,
They live on crispy pancakes
    Of yellow tide foam;
Some in the reeds
    Of the black mountain lake,
With frogs as their watchdogs,
    All night awake.

High on the hilltop
    The old King sits;
He's now so old and grey
    He's nigh lost his wits
With a bridge of white mist
    Columbkill he crosses,
On his stately journeys
From Slieveleague to Rosses;
Or going up with music
    On cold starry nights,
To sup with the queen
    Of the gay Northern Lights.

They stole little Bridget
    For seven years long;
When she came down again
    Her friends were all gone.
They took her lightly back,
    Between the night and morrow,
They thought that she was fast asleep,
    But she was dead with sorrow.
They have kept her ever since
    Deep within the lake,
On a bed of flag-leaves
    Watching till she wake.

By the craggy hillside,
    Through the mosses bare,
They have planted thorn trees
    For pleasure here and there.
Is any man so daring
    As dig them up in spite,
He shall find their sharpest thorns
    In his bed at night.

Up the airy mountain,
    Down the rushy glen,
We daren't go a-hunting
    For fear of little men;
Wee folk, good folk,
    Trooping all together;
Green jacket, red cap,
    And white owl's feather!

Columbkill = Glencolumbkille, a long glen in southwest Donegal; flag-leaves = leaves of wild iris.

When I Set Out for Lyonnesse

Thomas Hardy (1840–1928)

Written in 1868 after the poet's return from St Joliot in Cornwall where
he met Emma Gifford, who afterwards became his wife.

When I set out for Lyonnesse,
   A hundred miles away,
   The rime was on the spray,
And starlight lit my lonesomeness
When I set out for Lyonnesse
   A hundred miles away.

What would bechance at Lyonnesse
   While I should sojourn there
   No prophet durst declare,
Nor did the wisest wizard guess
What would bechance at Lyonnesse
   While I should sojourn there.

When I came back from Lyonnesse
   With magic in my eyes,
   All marked with mute surmise
My radiance rare and fathomless,
When I came back from Lyonnesse
   With magic in my eyes.

Lyonnesse = the drowned land between Cornwall and Scilly, the scene
of King Arthur's last battle

Ode

Arthur O'Shaughnessy (1844-81)

We are the music makers,
    And we are the dreamers of dreams,
Wandering by lone sea-breakers,
    And sitting by desolate streams –
World-losers and world-forsakers,
    On whom the pale moon dreams:
Yet we are the movers and shakers
    Of the world for ever, it seems.

With wonderful deathless ditties
We build up the world's great cities,
    And out of a fabulous story
    We fashion an empire's glory:
One man with a dream, at pleasure,
    Shall go forth and conquer a crown;
And three with a new song's measure
    Can trample a kingdom down.

We, in the ages lying
    In the buried past of the earth,
Built Nineveh with our sighing
    And Babel itself in our mirth;
And o'erthrew them with prophesying
    To the old of the new world's worth;
For each age is a dream that is dying
    Or one that is coming to birth.

A Ship, an Isle, a Sickle Moon (1913)

James Elroy Flecker (1884–1915)

A ship, an isle, a sickle moon –
With few but with how splendid stars
The mirrors of the sea are strewn
Between the silver bars!

An isle beside an isle she lay,
The pale ship anchored in the bay,
While in the young moon's port of gold
A star-ship – as the mirrors told –
Put forth its great and lonely light
To the unreflecting Ocean, Night.
And still, a ship upon her seas,
The isle and the island cypresses
Went sailing on without the gale:
And still there moved the moon so pale,
A crescent ship without a sail!

The Humour o' It

Civitas Ardmachana

Archbishop Octavian del Palatio (app. to Armagh in 1480)

Civitas Ardmachana,
Civitas vana,
Absque bonis moribus;
Mulieres nudae,
Carnes crudae
Paupertas in aedibus.

[Armagh folk – what a pity!
Think their wee town's a city
And with rudeness are patently swellin';
Their women go bare
They eat their meat rare
And their houses are not fit to dwell in.]

A Bhean Lán de Stuaim
[O Woman full of tricks]

Seathrún Céitinn (c. 1580–1644)

An ironical farewell to the pleasures of the flesh by a doctor of divinity

A bhean lán de stuaim
coingibh uaim do lámh;
ní fear gníomha sinn,
cé taoi tinn dar ngrádh.

Féach a liath dem fholt,
féach mo chorp gan lúth,
féach ar traoch dem fhuil –
créad re bhfuil do thnúth?

Ná saoil mé go saobh,
  arís ná claon do cheann;
bíodh ar ngrádh gan gníomh
  go bráth, a shíodh seang.

Druid do bhéal óm bhéal –
  doiligh an scéal do chor –
ná bíom cneas re cneas:
  tig ón teas an tol.

Do chúl craobhach cás
  do rosc glas mar dhrúcht,
do chíoch chruinngheal bláith,
  tharraingeas mian súl.

Gach gníomh acht gníomh cuirp
  is luighe id chuilt shuain
do-ghéan féin tréd ghrádh,
  a bhean lán de stuaim.

[Foxy lady! keep your hands to yourself; no matter how hot *you*
may be I'm past it!

Look at my grey thatch, my saggy frame; the old blood's too
thin. What are you at!

I'm not being awkward; so don't shake that head. Couldn't we
be just friends from now on, you slinky witch?

Take your lips from mine; you're overheated and I can't afford
to touch that skin in case I catch fire too.

Your Pre-Raphaelite hair, your eyes soft as dew, your flowery
breasts – all dazzle my eyes.

I'll do anything you ask, you lovely wily woman – except that
one thing!]

Out upon It, I Have Loved

Sir John Suckling (1609–42)

Out upon it, I have lov'd
    Three whole days together;
And am like to love three more,
    If it prove fair weather.

Time shall moult away his wings
    Ere he shall discover
In the whole wide world again
    Such a constant lover.

But the spite on't is, no praise
    Is due at all to me:
Love with me had made no stays
    Had it any been but she.

Had it any been but she
    And that very face,
There had been at least ere this
    A dozen dozen in her place.

On Marriage

Thomas Flatman (1637–88)

How happy a thing were a wedding,
   And a bedding,
If a man might purchase a wife
   For a twelvemonth and a day;
But to live with her all a man's life,
   For ever and for aye,
Till she grow as grey as a cat,
Good faith, Mr Parson, I thank you for that.

On Charles II

John Wilmot, Earl of Rochester (1647–80)

Here lies our mutton-eating king
Whose word no man relies on
Who never said a foolish one,
Nor ever did a wise one.

Charles's response was: 'My sayings are my own; my actions are my ministers'.'

[from] Verses on the Death of Dr Swift

Jonathan Swift (1667–1745)

Written by himself in November 1731

....

My female friends whose tender hearts
Have better learn'd to act their parts,
Receive the news in doleful dumps,
'The Dean is dead, (and what is trumps?)
Then, Lord have mercy on his soul.
(Ladies, I'll venture for the vole.)
Six deans they say must bear the pall.
(I wish I knew what king to call.)
Madam, your husband will attend
The funeral of so good a friend.
No madam, 'tis a shocking sight,
And he's engaged tomorrow night!
My Lady Club would take it ill,
If he should fail her at quadrille.
He lov'd the Dean. (I lead a heart.)
But dearest friends, they say, must part.
His time has come; he ran his race;
We hope he's in a better place.'

....

'He gave what little wealth he had
To build a house for fools and mad:
And showed by one satiric touch,
No nation wanted it so much:
That kingdom he has left his debtor,
I wish it soon may have a better.'

vole = a contract to obtain all the tricks in the game of quadrille

Expected Rhymes

Alexander Pope (1688–1744)

From *An Essay in Criticism* (1709)

Where-e'er you find *the cooling Western Breeze*,
In the next Line, it *whispers thro' the Trees*
If *Chrystal Streams with pleasing Murmurs creep,*
The Reader's threatened (not in vain) with *Sleep.*

On Certain Ladies

Alexander Pope (1688–1744)

When other fair ones to the shades go down,
Still Chloe, Flavia, Delia, stay in town:
Those ghosts of beauty wandering here reside,
And haunt the places where their honour died.

Prescription

Anon (18th Century)

A lady lately, that was fully sped
Of all the pleasures of the marriage bed
Ask'd a physician, whether were more fit
For Venus' sports, the morning or the night?
The good old man made answer, as 'twas meet,
The morn more wholesome, but the night more sweet.
May then, i'faith, quoth she, since we have leisure,
We'll to't each morn for health, each night for pleasure.

On Prince Frederick

Anon (18th Century)

Squib about Frederick Louis, Prince of Wales (1707–1751) who died
before his father George I

Here lies Fred,
Who was alive and is dead.
Had it been his father,
I had much rather;
Had it been his brother,
Still better than another;
Had it been his sister,
No one would have miss'd her;
Had it been the whole generation,
Still better for the nation;
But since 'tis only Fred,
Who was alive and is dead,
There's no more to be said.

Elegy on the Death of a Mad Dog

Oliver Goldsmith (1728–74)

Good people all, of every sort,
    Give ear unto my song;
And if you find it wond'rous short
    It cannot hold you long.

In Islington there was a man,
    Of whom the world might say,
That still a godly race he ran,
    Whene'er he went to pray.

A kind and gentle heart he had,
    To comfort friends and foes;
The naked every day he clad
When he put on his clothes.

And in that town a dog was found
    As many dogs there be,
Both mongrel, puppy, whelp and hound,
    And curs of low degree.

The dog and man at first were friends;
    But when a pique began,
The dog to gain some private ends,
    Went mad and bit the man.

Around from all the neighbouring streets
    The wond'ring neighbours ran,
And swore the dog had lost its wits,
    To bite so good a man.

The wound it seemed both sore and sad
    To every christian eye;
And while they swore the dog was mad,
    They swore the man would die.

But soon a wonder came to light,
    That showed the rogues they lied:
The man recovered of the bite,
    The dog it was that died.

Ireland Never Was Contented

Walter Savage Landor (1775–1864)

Ireland never was contented.
Say you so? You are demented.
Ireland was contented when
All could use the sword and pen,
And when Tara rose so high
That her turret split the sky,
And about her courts were seen
Liveried angels robed in green,
Wearing, by St Patrick's bounty,
Emeralds big as half the county.

The Four Georges

Walter Savage Landor (1775–1864)

George the First was always reckon'd
Vile – but viler George the Second;
And what mortal ever heard
Any good of George the Third?
When from earth the Fourth descended
God be praised, the Georges ended.

The Crime

Richard Monckton-Milnes, 1st Baron Houghton (1809–85)

On the first of September, one Sunday morn
I shot a hen pheasant in standing corn
Without a licence. Contrive who can
Such a cluster of crimes against God and man!

A Tragic Story

William Makepeace Thackeray (1811–63)

There lived a sage in days of yore,
And he a handsome pigtail wore:
But wondered much and sorrowed more,
Because it hung behind him.

He mused upon this curious case,
And swore he'd change the pigtail's place,
And have it dangling in his face,
Not dangling there behind him.

Says he, 'The mystery I've found –
I'll turn me round' – he turned him round;
But still it hung behind him.

Then round, and round, and out and in,
All day the puzzled sage did spin;
In vain – it mattered not a pin –
The pigtail hung behind him.

And though his efforts ever slack,
And though he twist, and turn, and tack,
Alas still faithful to his back,
The pigtaii hangs behind him.

My Last Duchess

Robert Browning (1812–89)

That's my last Duchess painted on the wall,
Looking as if she were alive. I call
That piece a wonder, now: Frà Pandolf's hands
Worked busily a day, and there she stands.
Will't please you sit and look at her? I said
'Frà Pandolf' by design: for never read
Strangers like you that pictured countenance,
The depth and passion of its earnest glance,
But to myself they turned (since none puts by
The curtain I have drawn for you, but I)
And seemed as they would ask me, if they durst,
How such a glance came there; so, not the first
Are you to turn and ask thus. Sir, 'twas not
Her husband's presence only, called that spot
Of joy into the Duchess' cheek: perhaps
Frà Pandolf chanced to say, 'Her mantle laps
Over my lady's wrist too much,' or 'Paint
Must never hope to reproduce the faint
Half-flush that dies along her throat:' such stuff
Was courtesy, she thought, and cause enough
For calling up that spot of joy. She had
A heart – how shall I say? – too soon made glad,
Too easily impressed; she liked whate'er
She looked on, and her looks went everywhere.
Sir, 't was all one! My favour at her breast,
The dropping of the daylight in the West,

The bough of cherries some officious fool
Broke in the orchard for her, the white mule
She rode with round the terrace – all and each
Would draw from her alike the approving speech,
Or blush, at least. She thanked men, – good! but
    thanked
Somehow – I know not how – as if she ranked
My gift of a nine-hundred-years-old name
With anybody's gift. Who'd stoop to blame
This sort of trifling? Even had you skill
In speech – (which I have not) – to make your will
Quite clear to such an one, and say, 'Just this
Or that in you disgusts me; here you miss,
Or there exceed the mark' – and if she let
Herself be lessoned so, nor plainly set
Her wits to yours, forsooth, and made excuse,
– E'en then would be some stooping; and I choose
Never to stoop. Oh, sir, she smiled, no doubt,
Whene'er I passed her; but who passed without
Much the same smile? This grew; I gave commands;
Then all smiles stopped together. There she stands
As if alive. Will 't please you rise? We'll meet
The company below then. I repeat,
The Count your master's known munificence
Is ample warrant that no just presence
Of mine for dowry will be disallowed;
Though his fair daughter's self, as I avowed
As starting, is my object. Nay, we'll go
Together down, sir. Notice Neptune, though,
Taming a sea horse, thought a rarity,
Which Claus of Innsbruck cast in bronze for me!

A Piece of Toast

James Payn (1830–98)

Parody of lines about a 'dear gazelle' from *Lalla Rookh* (1817) by
Thomas Moore (1779–1852) published in *Chamber's Journal* on 2
February 1884

I had never had a piece of toast
Particularly long and wide,
But fell upon the sanded floor,
And always on the buttered side.

Ballad

Charles Stuart Calverley (1831–84)

The auld wife sat at her ivied door
   (Butter and eggs and a pound of cheese)
A thing she had frequently done before;
   And her spectacles lay on her aproned knees.

The piper he piped on the hilltop high,
   (Butter and eggs and a pound of cheese)
Till the cow said, 'I die,' and the goose asked 'why?'
   And the dog said nothing, but searched for fleas.

The farmer he strode through the square farmyard;
   (Butter and eggs and a pound of cheese)
His last brew of ale was a trifle hard –
   The connexion of which with the plot one sees.

The farmer's daughter hath frank blue eyes
    (Butter and eggs and a pound of cheese)
She hears the rooks caw in the windy skies,
    As she sits at her lattice and shells her peas.

The farmer's daughter hath ripe red lips;
    (Butter and eggs and a pound of cheese)
If you try to approach her she skips
    Over tables and chairs with apparent ease.

The farmer's daughter hath soft brown hair;
    (Butter and eggs and a pound of cheese)
And I met with a ballad, I can't tell where,
    Which wholly consisted of lines like these.

She sat with her hands 'neath her dimpled cheeks,
    (Butter and eggs and a pound of cheese)
And spake not a word. When a lady speaks
    There is hope, but she didn't even sneeze.

She sat with her hands 'neath her crimson cheeks
    (Butter and eggs and a pound of cheese)
She gave up mending her father's breeks,
    And let the cat roll in her new chemise.

She sat with her hands 'neath her burning cheeks
    (Butter and eggs and a pound of cheese)
And gazed at the piper for thirteen weeks;
    Then she followed him out o'er the misty leas.

Her sheep followed her, as their tails did them
    (Butter and eggs and a pound of cheese)
And this song is considered a perfect gem,
    And as to the meaning, it's what you please.

Rigid Body Sings

James Clerk Maxwell (1831–79)

Physicist's parody of 'Comin thro' the Rye' by Robert Burns (see p161)

Gin a body meet a body
    Flyin' through the air,
Gin a body hit a body,
    Will it fly and where?
Ilka impact has its measure,
    Ne'er a'ane hae I
Yet a' the lads they measure me
    Or, at least, they try.

Gin a body meet a body
    Altogether free,
How they travel afterwards
    We do not always see.
Ilka problem has its method
    By analytics high;
For me I ken na ane o'them
    But what the waur am I?

waur = worse

*[from] The Queen's After-dinner Speech
(as overheard and Cut into lengths of Poetry by
Jamesy Murphy, Deputy-Assistant-Waiter at the
Viceregal Lodge, AD 1900)*

Percy French (1852–1920)

'Me loving subjects,' sez she,
'Here's me best respects,' sez she,
'An I'm proud this day,' sez she,
'Of the illigant way,' sez she,
'Ye gave me the hand,' sez she,
'Whin I came to land,' sez she,
'There was some people said,' sez she,
'They was greatly in dread,' sez she,
'I'd be moidered or shot,' sez she,
'As like as not,' sez she,
'But 'tis mighty clear,' sez she,
"Tis not over here,' sez she,
'I have cause to fear,' sez she,
"Tis them Bulgruins,' sez she,
'That's throwing bombs,' sez she,
'And scarin' the life,' sez she,
'Out of me son and the wife,' sez she,
'But in these parts,' sez she,
'They have warrum hearts,' sez she,
'And they like me well,' sez she,
'Barrin' Anna Parnell,' sez she,
'And that other wan,' sez she,
'That Maud Gonne,' sez she,
'Dhressin' in black,' sez she,
'To welcome me back,' sez she,
Though I don't care,'
An' all that gammon,' sez she,
'About me bringin' the famine, sez she,
'Now Maud'll write,' sez she,

'That I brought the blight,' sez she,
'Or altered the saysons' sez she,
'For political raysons' sez she,
'An' I think there's a slate,' sez she,
'Off Willie Yeats,' sez she,
'He should be at home,' sez she,
'French polishin' a pome,' sez she,
An' not writin' letters,' sez she,
'About his betters,' sez she,
'Paradin' me crimes,' sez she,
'In the *Irish Times*,' sez she, . . .

Victoria visited Dublin in April 1900 and stayed three weeks; it was
only two years since her jubilee visit and the 1798 centenary Nationalist
agitation, partly organised by Maud Gonne (and a lukewarm Yeats),
was still strong; Anna Parnell (1852–1911) was sister of the lost Irish
leader and founder of the Ladies Land League

She Was One of the Early Birds

T.W. Connor

Song made famous by the music-hall artist George Beauchamp (1863–
1901) in the 1880s. Nothing is now known of the author.

It was at the pantomime
Sweet Mabel and I did meet.
She was in the ballet (front row)
And I in a five-shilling seat:
She was dressed like a dicky bird
Beautiful; wings she had on,
Figure divine, wished she were mine;
On her I was totally gone.

Chorus (to be repeated after each verse):
> She was a dear little dicky bird
> 'Chip, chip, chip,' she went.
> Sweetly she sang to me
> Till all my money was spent
> Then she went off song;
> We parted on fighting terms;
> She was one of the early birds
> And I was one of the worms.

At the stage-door ev'ry night
I waited with my bouquet
Till my bird had moulted, and then,
We'd drive in a hansom away.
Oyster suppers and sparkling 'Cham'
Couldn't she go it! What ho!
Fivers I spent; tenners I lent
For to her I couldn't say, 'No!'

Eelskin coats and diamond rings
Knocked holes in my purse alone.
She would have them and in the end
I got hers by pawning my own.
When at last I was fairly broke,
'Twixt us a quarrel arose;
Mabel the fair pulled out my hair
And clawed all the skin off my nose.

Full of love and poverty
And armed with a carving knife,
One dark night I knelt in the mud
And asked if she'd be my wife.
Something struck me behind the ear;
Someone said, 'Now go and get
A wife of your own; leave me alone.'
And that was the last time we met.

Poor 'Biby'

Anon (late 19th Century)

A muvver was barfin' 'er biby one night,
The youngest of ten and a tiny young mite,
The muvver was poor and the biby was thin,
Only a skelington covered in skin:
The muvver turned rahnd for the soap off the rack,
She was but a moment, but when she turned back,
The biby was gorn: and in anguish she cried,
'Oh, where is my biby?' – The angels replied:

'Your biby 'as fell dahn the plug-'ole
Your biby 'as gorn dahn the plug;
The poor little thing was so skinny and thin
'E oughter been barfed in a jug;
Your biby is perfeckly 'appy,
'E won't need a barf any more,
Your biby 'as fell dahn the plug-'ole,
Not lorst, but gorn before.'

The Irish Pig

Anon (Early 20th Century)

'Twas an evening in November,
As I very well remember,
I was strolling down the street in drunken pride,
But my knees were all a'flutter
So I landed in the gutter,
And a pig came up and lay down by my side.

Yes I lay there in the gutter
Thinking thoughts I couldn't utter,
When a colleen passing by did softly say,
'Ye can tell a man that boozes
By the company he chooses.' –
At that, the pig got up and walked away!

Spring in Brooklyn NY

Anon (20th Century)

Der spring is sprung
Der grass is riz
I wonder where dem boidies is?

Der little boids is on der wing,
Ain't dat absoid?
Der little wings is on der boid!

The State of Man

Salve Regina

[attrib.] Aimar, Bishop of Le Puy (c. 1087)

Hymn to the Blessed Virgin by an author of whom little is known

Salve, regina, mater misericordiae,
Vita, dulcedo et spes nostra, salve!
Ad te clamamus exsules filii Evae,
Ad te suspiramus gementes et flentes
In hac lacrimarum valle.
Eia ergo, advocata nostra,
Illos tuos misericordes oculos ad nos converte.
Et Iesum, benedictum fructis ventris tui,
Nobis post hoc exilium ostende,
O clemens, o pia,
O dulcis virgo Maria.

[Hail holy queen, mother of mercy, hail our life, our sweetness and our hope. To thee do we cry, poor banished children of Eve; to thee do we send up our sighs, mourning and weeping in this vale of tears. Turn then most gracious advocate, thine eyes of mercy towards us; and after this our exile, show unto to us, the blessed fruit of thy womb, Jesus, O clement, O loving, O sweet virgin Mary.]

[from] Pange Lingua *(Speak, tongue)*

St Thomas Aquinas (1227–74)

Tantum ergo Sacramentum
Veneremur cernui,
Et antiquum documentum
Novo cedat ritui:
Praestet fides supplementum
Sensuum defectui.

Genitori, genitoque
Laus et jubilatio,
Salus, honor, virtus quoque
Sit et benedictio;
Procedenti ab utroque
Compar sit laudatio.

[Therefore prone in adoration we this great sacrament venerate, while the old order gives way to the new rite. Faith will hold, though our senses fail.

For creator and created let there be joy and jubilation; salvation, honour, strength and blessing on them; let equal praise be given to the one who is of both.]

[from] Lament for the Makaris (when he wes seik)

William Dunbar (?1460–?1520)

Lament for fellow poets by the chief lyricist of his time; the poem is
long and memorialises among others, Chaucer, John Gower (?1330–
1408) and fellow Scots, John Barbour (*c.* 1320–95), Robert Henrysoun
(*c.* 1420–*c.* 1490) and Blin Hary the Minstrel (fl. *c.* 1460-90)

I that in heill wes and gladness
Am trublit now with gret seikness
And feblit with infermitie:
Timor mortis conturbat me.

Our plesance here is all vain glory,
This fause warld is but transitory;
The flesh is brukle, the Feind is slee:
Timor mortis conturbat me.

The state of man dois change and vary,
Now sound, now seik, now blyth, now sary,
Now dansand mery, now like to dee:
Timor mortis conturbat me.

No state in eard here standis sickir;
As with the wynd wavis the wicker,
Wavis this warldis vanitee:
Timor mortis conturbat me.

....

Sen he hes all my brether tane
He will nocht let me live alane
On forse I man his nixt prey be:
Timor mortis conturbat me.

Sen for the deid remeid is none,
Best is that we for deid dispone,
Eftir our deid that live may we:
Timor mortis conturbat me.

makaris = poets; *Timor* etc = the dread of death agitates me; brukle =
frail; slee = crafty; sickir = certain; dispone = prepare

The Burning Babe

Robert Southwell (1561–95)

Famous lyric written by the Jesuit martyr who was beatified by Pius
XI

As I in hoary winter's night stood shivering in the
    snow,
Surprised I was with sudden heat which made my
    heart to glow:
And lifting up a fearful eye to view what fire was near,
A pretty babe all burning bright did in the air appear;
Who, scorchèd with excessive heat, such flood of tears
    did shed,
As though his floods should quench his flames with
    which his tears were fed.
'Alas!' quoth he, 'but newly born in fiery heats I fry,
Yet none approach to warm their hearts or feel my fire
    but I.
My faultless breast the furnace is, the fuel wounding
    thorns;
Love is the fire, and sighs the smoke, the ashes shame
    and scorns;
The fuel justice layeth on, and mercy blows the coals;
The metal in this furnace wrought are men defilèd
    souls:

For which, as now on fire I am to work them to their
     good,
So will I melt into a bath to wash them in my blood.'
With this he vanished out of sight and swiftly sunk
     away,
And straight I callèd unto mind that it was Christmas
     Day.

Insubstantial Pageant

William Shakespeare (1564–1616)

From *The Tempest* (1612)

Our revels now are ended. These our actors,
As I foretold you, were all spirits and
Are melted into air, into thin air:
And, like the baseless fabric of this vision,
The cloud-capp'd towers, the gorgeous palaces,
The solemn tempests, the great globe itself,
Yea, all which it inherit, shall dissolve
And, like this in substantial pageant faded,
Leave not a rack behind. We are such stuff
As dreams are made on, and our little life
Is rounded with a sleep.

In Time of Pestilence

Thomas Nashe (1567–1601)

Poem written in 1592 as part of the comedy *Summer's Last Will and Testament*

Adieu, farewell earth's bliss!
This world uncertain is:
Fond are life's lustful joys,
Death proves them all but toys.
None from his darts can fly;
I am sick, I must die –
    Lord, have mercy on us!

Rich men, trust not in wealth,
Gold cannot buy you health;
Physic himself must fade;
All things to end are made;
The plague full swift goes by;
I am sick, I must die –
    Lord, have mercy on us!

Beauty is but a flower
Which wrinkles will devour;
Brightness falls from the air;
Queens have died young and fair;
Dust hath closed Helen's eye;
I am sick, I must die –
    Lord, have mercy on us!

Strength stoops unto the grave,
Worms feed on Hector brave;
Swords may not fight with fate;
Earth still holds ope her gate;
Come, come! the bells do cry;
I am sick, I must die –
    Lord, have mercy on us!

Wit with his wantonness
Tasteth death's bitterness;
Hell's executioner
Hath no ears for to hear
With vain art can reply;
I am sick, I must die –
    Lord, have mercy on us!

Haste therefore each degree
To welcome destiny;
Heaven is our heritage,
Earth but a player's stage
Mount we unto the sky;
I am sick, I must die –
    Lord, have mercy on us!

And Did Those Feet

William Blake (1757–1827)

And did those feet in ancient time
Walk upon England's mountains green?
And was the holy lamb of God
On England's pleasant pastures seen?

And did the Countenance Divine
Shine forth upon our clouded hills?
And was Jerusalem builded here
Among these dark Satanic mills?

Bring me my bows of burning gold!
Bring me my arrows of desire!
Bring me my spear: O clouds unfold!
Bring me my chariot of fire!

I will not cease from mental fight
Nor shall my sword sleep in my hand
Till we have built Jerusalem
In England's green and pleasant land.

Surprised By Joy (1815)

William Wordsworth (1770–1850)

Written on the death of one of his children, 1815

Surprised by joy – impatient as the wind –
I turned to share the transport – O with whom
But Thee – deep buried in the silent tomb,
That spot that no vicissitude can find?
Love, faithful love, recalled thee to my mind –
But how could I forget thee? Through what power
Even for the least division of an hour
Have I been so beguiled as to be blind
To my most grievous loss – That thought's return
Was the worst pang that sorrow ever bore
Save one, only one, when I stood forlorn,
Knowing my heart's best treasure was no more;
That neither present time nor years unborn
Could to my sight that heavenly face restore.

Jenny Kiss'd Me (1838)

Leigh Hunt (1784–1859)

Poetic compliment to Jane Welsh whose marriage to Thomas Carlyle
made 'two people miserable instead of four' according to Samuel Butler

Jenny kiss'd me when we met
    Jumping from the chair she sat in;
Time you thief, who love to get
    Sweets into your list, put that in!
Say I'm weary, say I'm sad,
    Say that health and wealth have miss'd me,
Say I'm growing old, but add,
    Jenny kiss'd me.

So We'll Go No More A-Roving (1817)

George Gordon, Lord Byron (1788–1824)

So we'll go no more a-roving
    So late into the night,
Though the heart be still as loving,
    And the moon be still as bright.

For the sword outwears its sheath,
    And the soul outwears the breast,
And the heart must pause to breathe,
    And love itself have rest.

Though the night was made for loving,
    And the day returns too soon,
Yet we'll go no more a-roving
    By the light of the moon.

Tartar

Solyman Brown (1790–?1865)

One of several dental poems by an author of whom little else is known.

If sloth or negligence the task forbear
Of making cleanliness a daily care;
If fresh ablution, with the morning sun,
Be quite forborne or negligently done;
In dark disguise insidious tartar comes,
Incrusts the teeth and irritates the gums,
Till vile deformity usurps the seat
Where smiles should play and winning graces meet,
And foul disease pollutes the fair domain,
Where health and purity should ever remain.

When I Have Fears

John Keats (1795-1821)

When I have fears that I may cease to be
Before my pen has glean'd my teeming brain,
Before high-pilèd books, in charactr'y,
Hold like rich garners the full ripen'd grain;
When I behold upon the night's starr'd face,
Huge cloudy symbols of a high romance,
And feel that I may never live to trace
Their shadows with the magic hand of chance;
And when I feel, fair creature of an hour!
That I shall never look upon thee more
Never have relish in the faery power
Of unreflecting love; – then on the shore
  Of the wide world I stand alone, and think,
  Till love and fame to nothingness do sink.

Lead, Kindly Light

John Henry, Cardinal Newman (1801–90)

Written by Newman on 16 June 1833 on an orange boat bound for
Marseilles while convalescent and becalmed between Corsica and
Sardinia

Lead, kindly Light, amid the encircling gloom,
    Lead thou me on;
The night is dark, and I am far from home
    Lead thou me on.
Keep thou my feet; I do not wish to see
The distant scene; one step enough for me.

I was not ever thus, nor prayed that thou
    Shoulds't lead me on;
I loved to choose and see my path; but now
    Lead thou me on.
I loved the garish day, and, spite of fears,
Pride ruled my will: remember not past years.

So long thy power has blest me, sure it still
    Will lead me on
O'er moor and fen, o'er crag and torrent, till
    The night is gone,
And with the morn those angel faces smile,
Which I have loved long since, and lost awhile.

Say Not the Struggle Nought Availeth (1855)

Arthur Hugh Clough (1819–61)

Say not the struggle nought availeth,
    The labour and the wounds are vain,
The enemy faints not, nor faileth,
    And as things have been they remain.

If hopes were dupes, fears may be liars;
    It may be, in yon smoke conceal'd
Your comrades chase e'en now the fliers,
    And, but for you, possess the field.

For while the tired waves, vainly breaking,
    Seem here no painful inch to gain,
Far back, through creeks and inlets making,
    Come silent, flooding in, the main.

And not by eastern windows only,
    When daylight comes, comes in the light:
In front the sun climbs slow, how slowly!
    But westward, look, the land is bright!

Dover Beach

Matthew Arnold (1822–88)

Partly written on his honeymoon with Fanny Lucy Wightman in 1851

The sea is calm tonight
The tide is full, the moon lies fair
Upon the Straits; – on the French coast, the light
Gleams and is gone; the cliffs of England stand,
Glimmering and vast, out in the tranquil bay.
Come to the window, sweet is the night air!
Only, from the long line of spray
Where the sea meets the moon-blanched land,
Listen! you hear the grating roar
Of pebbles which the waves draw back, and fling,
At their return, up the high strand,
Begin, and cease, and then again begin,
With tremulous cadence slow, and bring
The eternal note of sadness in.

Sophocles long ago
Heard it on the Aegean, and it brought
Into his mind the turbid ebb and flow
Of human misery; we
Find also in the sound a thought,
Hearing it by this distant northern sea.

The sea of faith
Was once, too, at the full, and round earth's shore
Lay like the folds of a bright girdle furled;
But now I only hear
Its melancholy, long, withdrawing roar,
Retreating to the breath
Of the night-wind down the vast edges drear
And naked shingles of the world.

Ah, love, let us be true
To one another! for the world which seems
To lie before us like a land of dreams,
So various, so beautiful, so new,
Hath really neither joy, nor love, nor light,
Nor certitude, nor peace, nor help for pain;
And we are here as on a darkling plain
Swept with confused alarms of struggle and flight,
Where ignorant armies clash by night.

Up-Hill

Christina Rossetti (1830–94)

Does the road wind up-hill all the way?
    Yes, to the very end.
Will the day's journey take the whole long day?
    From morn to night, my friend

But is there for the night a resting-place,
    A roof when the slow, dark hours begin?
May not the darkness hide it from my face?
    You cannot miss the inn.

Shall I meet other wayfarers at night?
    Those who have gone before.
Then must I knock, or call when just in sight?
    They will not keep you waiting at the door.

Shall I find comfort, travel-sore and weak?
    Of labour you shall find the sum.
Will there be beds for me and all who seek?
    Yea, beds for all who come.

Gerard Manley Hopkins (1844–89)

Spiritual sonnet suggested by Jeremiah 12:1

Thou art indeed just, Lord, if I contend
With thee; but, sir, so what I plead is just.
Why do sinners' ways prosper? and why must
Disappoint all I endeavour end?
Wert thou my enemy, O thou my friend,
How wouldst thou worse, I wonder, than thou dost
Defeat, thwart me? Oh the sots and thralls of lust
Do in spare hours more thrive than I that spend,
Sir, life upon thy cause. See, banks and brakes
Now, leavéd how thick, laced they are again
With fretty chevril, look, and fresh wind shakes
Them; birds build – but I do not build; no but strain,
Time's eunuch, and not breed one work that wakes.
Mine, O thou lord of life, send my roots rain.

Spring and Fall – to a young child

Gerard Manley Hopkins (1844–89)

Márgáret, áre you gríeving
Over Goldengrove unleaving?
Leáves, like the things of man, you
With your fresh thoughts care for, can you?
Áh! ás the heart grows older
It will come to such sights colder
By and by, nor spare a sigh
Though worlds of wanwood leafmeal lie;
And yet you *will* weep and know why.
Now no matter, child, the name:
Sórrow's springs áre the same.
Nor mouth had, no nor mind, expressed
What heart heard of, ghost guessed:
It is the blight man was born for,
It is Margaret you mourn for.

Out of the Night That Covers Me (1888)

W[illiam] E[rnest] Henley (1849–1903)

Out of the night that covers me,
    Black as the pit from pole to pole,
I thank whatever gods may be
    For my unconquerable soul

In the fell clutch of circumstance
    I have not winced nor cried aloud.
Under the bludgeonings of chance
    My head is bloody but unbow'd.

Beyond this place of wrath and tears
    Looms but the Horror of the shade,
And yet the menace of the years
    Finds and shall find me unafraid.

It matters not how strait the gate,
    How charged with punishments the scroll,
I am the master of my fate:
    I am the captain of my soul.

Alice Meynell (1852–1922)

One wept whose only child was dead,
New-born, ten years ago.
'Weep not; he is in bliss,' they said.
She answered, 'Even so,

'Ten years ago was born in pain
A child not now forlorn.
But oh, ten years ago, in vain,
A mother, a mother was born.

Vitae Summa Brevis Spem Nos Vetat Inchoare Longam
[The shortness of life forbids us to hope for long]

Ernest Dowson (1867–1900)

The Latin title, like that of the 'Cynara' poem (see p. 72) is from the first book of Horace's *Odes* (23 BC)

They are not long, the weeping and the laughter,
    Love and desire and hate:
I think they have no portion in us after
    We pass the gate.

They are not long, the days of wine and roses:
    Out of a misty dream
Our path emerges for a while, then closes
    Within a dream.

The Wayfarer

Padraic Pearse (1879–1916)

Written on the eve of his execution, 3 May 1916

The beauty of the world hath made me sad,
This beauty that will pass:
Sometimes my heart hath shaken with great joy
To see a leaping squirrel in a tree,
Or a red ladybird upon a stalk,
Or little rabbits in a field at evening,
Lit by a slanting sun,
Or some green hill where mountainy man hath sown
And soon will reap, near to the gate of Heaven;
Or children with bare feet upon the sands
Of some ebbed sea, or playing on the streets
Of little towns in Connacht,
Things young and happy.
And then my heart hath told me
These will pass,
Will pass, and change, will die and be no more,
Things bright and green, things young and happy;
And I have gone upon my way
Sorrowful.

Lament for the Poets: 1916

Francis Ledwidge (1887–1917)

Written in Ebrington Barracks, Derry, where Ledwidge had a home
posting between survival at Gallipoli and death in Belgium

I heard the Poor Old Woman say:
'At break of day the fowler came,
And took my blackbirds from their songs
Who loved me well thro' shame and blame.

'No more from lovely distances
Their songs shall bless me mile by mile
Nor to white Ashbourne call me down
To wear my crown another while.

'With bended flowers the angels mark
For the skylark the place they lie,
From there its little family
Shall dip their wings first in the sky.

'And when the first surprise of flight
Sweet songs excite, from the far dawn
Shall there come blackbirds loud with love,
Sweet echoes of the singers gone.

'But in the lonely hush of eve
Weeping I grieve the silent bills,'
I heard the Poor Old Woman say
In Derry of the little hills.

Green and Pleasant Land

Linden Lea

William Barnes (1801–86)

Written in Dorset dialect (the third verse began 'Let other vo'k mëake money vaster'), this poem was set to music by Vaughan Williams

Within the woodlands, flow'ry shaded
By the oak trees' mossy moot,
The shining grass blades, timber shaded,
Now do quiver under foot:
And birds do whistle overhead,
And water's bubbling in its bed;
And there for me
The apple tree
Do lean down low in Linden Lea.

When leaves, that lately were a-springing
Now do fade within the copse,
And painted birds do hush their singing,
Up upon the timber tops:
And brown-leaved fruit's a-turning red,
In cloudless sunshine overhead,
With fruit for me,
The apple tree
Do lean down low in Linden Lea.

Let other folk make money faster,
In the air of dark-room'd towns:
I don't dread a peevish master,
Though no man heed my frowns.
I be free to go abroad,
Or take again my homeward road.
To where, for me,
The apple tree
Do lean down low in Linden Lea.

Home Thoughts, from Abroad

Robert Browning (1812–89)

Oh! to be in England
Now that April's there,
And whoever wakes in England
Sees, some morning, unaware,
That the lowest boughs and the brushwood sheaf
Round the elm-tree bole are in tiny leaf,
While the chaffinch sings in the orchard bough
In England – now!
And after April, when May follows,
And the whitethroat builds, all the swallows!
Hark, where my blossomed pear-tree in the hedge
Leans to the field and scatters on the clover
Blossoms and dewdrops – at the bent spray's edge –
That's the wise thrush; he sings each song twice over,
Lest you should think he never could recapture
The first fine careless rapture!
And though the fields look rough with hoary dew,
All will be gay when noontide wakes anew
The buttercups, the little children's dower
– Far brighter than this gaudy melon-flower

Inversnaid

Gerard Manley Hopkins (1844–89)

This darksome burn, horseback brown,
His rollrock highroad roaring down,
In coop and comb the fleece of his foam
Flutes and low to the lake falls home.

A windpuff-bonnet of fáwn-fróth
Turns and twindles over the broth
Of a pool so pitchblack, féll-frówning,
In rounds and rounds despair to drowning.

Dagged with dew, dappled with dew
Are the groins of the braes that the brook treads
        through,
Wiry heathpacks, flitches of fern,
With the beadbonny ash that sits over the burn.

What would the world be, once bereft
Of wet and wildness? Let them be left,
O let them be left, wildness and wet;
Long live the weeds and the wildness yet.

William Larminie (1850–1890)

Quiet are the treeless hills
Clad with short coarse grass and heather;
Around them the sky's wide circle
And beneath them the silent sea.

And around the sky's wide circle are clouds of fire,
Towers of flaming snow;
And the plain of the gleaming sea reflects the glitter
In lonely patches of calm.

Wild fiery-splendid sky!
Silent protest of day against night's dark domination,
Over thy splendour already hangeth the omen of
      gloom.
And the sea inscrutable rests, vast levels of flickering
      darkness,
Watching the sunset go:
All day to the sky it has spoken and in brightness
      answered to brightness,
Now will it speak to the night.

If there is gloom in the heaven
Shall not the gloom of hell be twice intense?
Therefore ye faces rise!
Ye that within the sunless depths have dwellings,
And by the deeper terror of your eyes
Smite the night's heart with trembling.

The Dead at Clonmacnoise
(from the Irish of Angus Ó Giolláin)

Thomas William Rolleston (1857–1920)

In a quiet water'd land, a land of roses,
 Stands Saint Kieran's city fair;
And the warriors of Erin in their famous generations
 Slumber there.

There beneath the dewy hillside sleep the noblest
 Of the clan of Conn,
Each below his stone with name in branching Ogham
 And the sacred knot thereon

And in Clonmacnoise they laid the men of Teffra,
 And right many a lord of Breagh;
Deep the sod above Clan Creide and Clan Conaill,
 Kind in hall and fierce in fray.

Many and many a son of Conn the Hundred-Fighter
 In the red earth lies at rest;
Many a blue eye of Clan Colman the turf covers,
 Many a swan-white breast.

The Little Waves of Breffny

Eva Gore-Booth (1870–1926)

The grand road from the mountain goes shining to the
    sea,
  And there is traffic in it and many a horse and cart,
But the little roads of Cloonagh are dearer far to me,
  And the little roads of Cloonagh go rambling
    through my heart.

A great storm from the ocean goes shouting o'er the
    hill,
  And there is glory in it and terror on the wind,
But the haunted air of twilight is very strange and still,
  And the little winds of twilight are dearer to my
    mind.

The great waves of the Atlantic sweep storming on the
    way,
  Shining green and silver with the hidden herring
    shoal,
But the Little Waves of Breffny have drenched my
    heart in spray,
  And the Little Waves of Breffny go stumbling
    through my soul.

John-John

Thomas MacDonagh (1878–1916)

I dreamt last night of you, John-John,
   And thought you called to me;
And when I woke this morning, John,
   Yourself I hoped to see;
But I was all alone, John-John,
   Though still I heard your call:
I put my boots and bonnet on
   And took my Sunday shawl,
And went full dure to find you, John,
               At Nenagh fair.

The fair was just the same as then,
   Five years ago today,
When first you left the thimble men
   And came with me away;
For there again were thimble men
   And shooting galleries,
And card-trick men and Maggie men
   Of all sorts and degrees –
But not a sight of you, John-John,
               Was anywhere.

I turned my face to home again,
   And called myself a fool
To think you'd leave the thimble men
   And live again by rule,
And go to Mass and keep the fast
   And till the patch:
My wish to have you home was past
   Before I raised the latch
And pushed the door and saw you, John
               Sitting down here.

How cool you came in here, begad,
    As if you owned the place!
But rest yourself there now, my lad,
    'Tis good to see your face;
My dream is out, and now by it
    I think I know my mind:
At six o'clock this house you'll quit,
    And leave no grief behind –
But until six o'clock, John-John,
            My bit you'll share.

The neighbour's shame of me began
    When first I brought you in
To wed and keep a tinker man
    They thought a kind of sin;
But now this three year since you're gone
    'Tis pity me they do,
And that I'd rather have, John-John
    Than that they'd pity you.
Pity for me and you, John-John
            I could not bear.

Oh, you're my husband right enough,
    But what's the good of that?
You know you never were the stuff
    To be the cottage cat,
To watch the fire and hear me lock
    The door and put out Shep –
But there now, it is six o'clock
    And time for you to step.
God bless and keep you far, John-John!
            And that's my prayer.

Maggie men = fairground showmen (from *margadh* = fair)

Adlestrop

Edward Thomas (1878–1917)

Adlestrop is no longer a railway station but the local people have attached the old GWR nameplate to the bus station.

Yes, I remember Adlestrop –
The name, because one afternoon
Of heat the express-train drew up there
Unwontedly. It was late June.

The steam hissed. Someone cleared his throat.
No one left and no one came
On the bare platform. What I saw
Was Adlestrop – only the name

And willows, willowherb, and grass,
And meadowsweet, and haycocks dry,
No whit less still and lonely fair
Than the high cloudlets in the sky.

And for that minute a blackbird sang
Close by, and round him, mistier,
Farther and farther, all the birds
Of Oxfordshire and Gloucestershire.

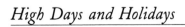
High Days and Holidays

[from] Confessio

The Arch-poet (fl. 1159–67)

Meum est propositum
In taberna mori,
Ut sint vina proxima
Morientis ori.
Tunc cantabunt laetius
Angelorum chori:
'Sit Deus propitius
Huic potatori!'

[My wish is to die in a tavern,
Where the wines are conveniently near
To my gullet as I hand my chips in
And the voices of angels are clear:
'May the good Lord look down in his mercy
On this guy who drank all the year!']

Tempus Est Iocundum *[from Carmina Burana]*

Anon (13th century)

Tempus est iocundum
o virgines,
modo congaudete
vos iuvenes
Chorus (repeated after each verse):
>   *O o totus floreo*
>   *iam amore virginali*
>   *totus ardeo,*
>   *novus novus amor*
>   *est, quo pereo.*

Cantat philomena
sic dulciter,
et modulans auditur
intus caleo

Flos est puellarum
quam diligo
et rosa rosarum
quam sepe video

Tua me confortat
promissio,
tua me deportat
negatio.

Tua mecum ludit
virginitas,
tua me detrudit
simplicitas

Sile, philomena
pro tempore,
surge cantilena
de pectore.

Tempore brumali
vir patiens,
animo vernali
lasciviens.

Veni, domicella,
cum gaudio
veni, veni, bella
iam pereo

Carmina Burana = anthology of medieval lyrics written in the monastery
of Benictbeuern in Upper Bavaria

[Lassies, now is the time for pleasure and the lads can
    join in too.
Chorus:
I bloom with desire for a maiden; I am totally on fire.
    It's a new, new love and it's killing me!
The nightingale sings this chorus so sweetly and I burn
    with desire when she reprises her song.
The girl that I love is the flower of them all and the
    rose of all roses as I've frequently seen.
Your virginity teases, your candour deflates.
Shut up, nightingale, for a while, until the song of my
    heart is heard.
I have tholed all winter long but now with the spring
    I'm ready for pleasure.
Come willingly with me, sweetheart; come, come, you
    beauty or I'll perish.]

The Irish Dancer

Anon (c. 1300)

One of the earliest of Hiberno-English poems

Ich am of Irlaunde,
Ant of the holy londe
    Of Irlaunde.

Gode sire, pray ich the,
For of saynte charité
Come ant daunce wyth me
    In Irlaunde.

[from] L'Allegro

John Milton (1608–74)

There let Hymen oft appear
In saffron robe, with taper clear,
And pomp and feast, and revelry,
With mask, and antique pageantry,
Such sights as youthful poets dream
On summer eves by haunted stream.
Then to the well-trod stage anon,
If Jonson's learnèd sock be on,
Or sweetest Shakespeare, fancy's child
Warble his native wood-notes wild,
And ever against eating cares
Lap me in soft Lydian airs
Married to immortal verse,
Such as the meeting soul may pierce
In notes, with many a winding bout
Of linkèd sweetness long drawn out,
With wanton heed and giddy cunning,
The melting voice through mazes running,
Untwisting all the chains that tie
The hidden soul of harmony.

Drinking

Abraham Cowley (1618–67)

The thirsty earth soaks up the rain,
And drinks and gapes for drink again;
The plants suck in the earth, and are
With constant drinking fresh and fair;
The sea itself (which one would think
Should have but little need of drink)
Drinks ten thousand rivers up,
So fill'd that they o'erflow the cup.
The busy Sun (and one would guess
By's drunken fiery face no less)
Drinks up the sea and when he's done
The Moon and Stars drink up the Sun.
They drink and dance by their own light,
They drink and revel all the night.
Nothing in Nature's sober found,
But an eternal health goes round.
Fill up the bowl, then, fill it high,
Fill all the glasses there, for why
Should every creature drink but I?
Why man of morals tell me why?

Sally in Our Alley

Henry Carey (1687–1743)

A shoemakers's apprentice making a holiday with his sweetheart treated her to the sights of Bedlam, the puppet shows, the flying chairs, and all the elegancies of Moorfields, whence, proceeding to the Farthing Pie House, he gave her a collation of buns, cheesecakes, gammon of bacon, stuffed beer and bottled ale, through all of which scenes the author dodged them.

Of all the girls that are so smart
   There's none like pretty Sally:
She is the darling of my heart,
   And she lives in our alley.
There is no lady in the land
   Is half so sweet as Sally;
She is the darling of my heart,
   And she lives in our alley.
Her father he makes cabbage-nets
   And through the streets does cry 'em
Her mother she sells laces long
   To such as please to buy 'em:
But sure such folks could ne'er beget
   So sweet a girl as Sally!
She is the darling of my heart,
   And she lives in our alley.

When she is by, I leave my work,
   I love her most sincerely;
My master comes like any Turk,
   And bangs me most severely –
But let him bang his bellyful,
   I'll bear it all for Sally
She is the darling of my heart,
   And she lives in our alley.

Of all the days that's in the week
    I dearly love but one day –
And that's the day that comes betwixt
    A Saturday and Monday:
For then I'm drest all in my best
    To walk abroad with Sally;
She is the darling of my heart,
    And she lives in our alley.

My master carries me to church,
    And often am I blamed
Because I leave him in the lurch
    As soon as text is named;
I leave the church in sermon-time
    And slink away to Sally
She is the darling of my heart,
    And she lives in our alley.

When Christmas comes about again
    O then I shall have money;
I'll hoard it up, and box and all
    I'll give it to my honey:
I wish it were ten thousand pound,
    I'd give it all to Sally:
She is the darling of my heart,
    And she lives in our alley.

My master and my neighbours all
    Make game of me and Sally,
And, but for her, I'd better be
    A slave and row a galley;
But when my seven long years are out
    O then I'll marry Sally –
And then we'll wed, and then we'll bed
    But not in our alley!

Oliver Goldsmith (1728–74)

From *The Deserted Village*

How often have I bless'd the coming day,
When toil remitting lent its turn to play,
And all the village train, from labour free,
Led up their sports beneath the spreading tree;
While many a pastime circled in the shade,
The young contending as the old survey'd;
And many a gambol frolick'd o'er the ground,
And sleights of art and feats of strength went round;
And still as each repeated pleasure tir'd
Succeeding sports the mirthful band inspir'd;
The dancing pair that simply sought renown,
By holding out to tire each other down;
The swain mistrustless of his smutted face,
While secret laughter tittered round the place;
The bashful virgin's sidelong looks of love,
The matron's glance that would those looks reprove:
These were thy charms, sweet village; sports like these,
With sweet succession taught e'en toil to please;
These round thy bowers their cheerful influence shed,
These were thy charms – But all these charms are fled.

Preab san ól [Pleasure in Drink]

Riocard Bairéid (1740–1819)

Is iomai slí sin do bhíos ag daoine
Ag cruinniú píosaí 's ag déanamh stóir,
'S a laghad a smaoiníos ar ghiorra 'n tsaoil seo
'S go mbeidh siad sínte faoi leac go fóill.
Más tiarna tíre, diúc nó rí thú,
Ní rachaidh pingin leat ag dul faoi bhfód,
Mar sin, 's dá bhrí sin, níl beart níos críonna
Ná bheith go sioraí ag cur preab san ól.

An long ar sáile níl cuan ná cearda
Nach gcaithfeadh cairde fud an domhain mhóir,
Ó ríocht na Spáinne 'gus suas Gibraltar,
'Gus insan áit a mbíonn an Grand Seigneur,
Le gach cargo ag líonadh málaí
Ní choinneadh an bás uaidh uair nó ló,
Mar sin, a chairde, níl beart níos fearr dúinn
Ná bheith mar táimid, ag cur preab san ól.

[There are many ways that folks get money,
Gather pennies and make a pile;
Yet little they reck how short their stay is –
Stretched under the stone in a little while.
Whether squire or duke or even king
Not one red cent can you take there.
Since that's the way, no better practice
Than carouse all night without a care.

The ship on the main that does its business
In every harbour the wild world o'er
From the land of Spain up to Gibraltar
Even to the home of the Grand Seigneur,
Should it make a fortune with every trip
Not one extra day can its cargoes buy.
So then, my friends, what better occupation
Than this – to drink the tavern dry.]

The Deserter

John Philpot Curran (1750–1817)

If sadly thinking,
With spirits sinking,
Could more than drinking
 My cares compose,
A cure for sorrow
From sighs I'd borrow,
And hope tomorrow
 Would end my woes.
But as in wailing
There's not availing,
And Death unfailing
 Will strike the blow,
Then for that reason,
And for a season,
Let us be merry
 Before we go.
To joy a stranger,
A way-worn ranger,
In every danger
 My course I've run;
Now hope all ending
And Death befriending,
His last aid lending,

My cares are done:
No more a rover,
Or hapless lover,
My griefs are over,
   My grass runs low;
Then for that reason,
And for a season,
Let us be merry
   Before we go!

Comin thro' the Rye

Robert Burns (1759–96)

Comin thro' the rye, poor body
   Comin thro' the rye,
She draigl't a' her petticoatie
   Comin thro' the rye.

Oh Jenny's a' weet, poor body,
   Jenny's seldom dry,
She draigl't a' her petticoatie
   Comin thro' the rye.

Gin a body meet a body
   Comin thro' the rye,
Gin a body kiss a body,
   Need a body cry!

Gin a body meet a body
   Comin thro' the glen:
Gin a body kiss a body!
   Need the warld ken!

gin = should

Auld Lang Syne *[Old long ago]*

Robert Burns (1759-96)

Should auld acquaintance be forgot,
    And never brought to min'?
Should auld acquaintance be forgot,
    And auld lang syne?

> *For auld lang syne, my dear,*
> *For auld lang syne*
> *We'll tak a cup o'kindness yet,*
> *For auld lang syne.*

And surely ye'll be your pint-stowp,
    And surely I'll be mine;
And we'll tak a cup o' kindness yet
    For auld lang syne.

We two hae run about the braes,
    And pu'd the gowans fine
But we've wandered mony a weary foot
    Sin auld lang syne.
We twa hae paidled i' the burn,
    From morning sun till dine;
But seas between us braid hae roared
    Sin auld lang syne.

And there's a hand, my trusty fiere,
    And gie's a hand o' thine
And we'll take a right guid-willie waught.
    For auld lang syne.

gowans = daisies; fiere = companion; guid-willie waught = hearty draught

The Spanish Lady

Anon (Late 18th Century)

As I walked down through Dublin City
At the hour of twelve in the night
Who should I spy but a Spanish Lady
Washing her feet by candlelight?
First she dipped them, then she dried them
Over a fire of ambery coal.
Never in all my life did I see
A maid so neat about the sole.

I stopped to peep, but the Watchman passed
And says: young fellow, the night is late
Get home to bed or I'll wrastle you
At a double trot through the Bridewell Gate!
So I waved a kiss to the Spanish Lady
Hot as the fire of cramesy coal.
I've seen dark maids, though never one
So white and neat about the sole.

O she's too rich for a Poddle-swaddy
With her tortoise comb and mantle fine,
A Hellfire buck would fit her better,
Drinking brandy and claret wine.
I'm just a decent College sizar
Poor as a sod of smouldery coal;
And how would I dress the Spanish Lady
And she so neat about the sole?

O, she'd make a mott for the Provost Marshal
Or a wife for the Mayor on his coach so high,
Or a queen for Andalusia
Kicking her heel in the Cardinal's eye.
I'm blue as cockles, brown as herrings
Over a grid of glimmery coal
And all because of the Spanish Lady
So mortial neat about the sole.

I wandered north, and I wandered south
By Golden Lane and Patrick's Close,
The Coombe, Smithfield and Stoneybatter,
Back to Napper Tandy's house.
Old age has laid its hand upon me
Cold as a fire of ashy coal
And where is the lovely Spanish Lady
And the maid so neat about the sole?

Bridewell = city lock-up; cramesy = crimson; Poddle-swaddy = private
soldier; Hellfire buck = member of the notorious Templeogue club;
mott = sweetheart

Beidh Aonach Amárach

Anon (19th Century)

Beidh aonach amárach i gContae an Chláir;
Beidh aonach amárach i gContae an Chláir;
Beidh aonach amárach i gContae an Chláir;
Cén mhaith dom é! Ní bheidh mé ann.

A mháithrín, an ligfidh tú chun aonaigh mé?
A mháithrín, an ligfidh tú chun aonaigh mé?
A mháithrín, an ligfidh tú chun aonaigh mé?
A mhuirnín ó, ná héiligh é.

Níl tú a deich ná a haon déag fós;
Níl tú a deich ná a haon déag fós;
Níl tú a deich ná a haon déag fós;
Nuair a bheidh tú a trí déag beidh tú mór.

[There's a fair tomorrow in County Clare
What's that to me: I won't be there.

Mammy will you let me go to the fair?
My darling girl, don't ask me that!

You're still only eleven years old;
When you're thirteen you'll be big enough.]

Four Ducks on a Pond

William Allingham (1824–1889)

Four ducks on a pond,
A grass-bank beyond
A blue sky of spring,
White clouds on the wing;
What a little thing
To remember for years –
To remember with tears!

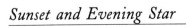

Sunset and Evening Star

'God be in My Head'

Sarum Missal (11th Century)

God be in my head
And in my understanding;

God be in my eyes,
And in my looking;

God be in my mouth,
And in my speaking;

God be in my heart,
And in my thinking

God be at my end,
And at my departing.

[from] Dies Irae

[attrib.] Thomas of Celano OFM (c. 1190–1260)

Dies irae, dies illa!
Solvet saeclum in favilla
Teste David cum Sibylla.

....

Tuba mirum spargens sonum
Per sepulchra regionum
Coget omnes ante thronum.

Mors stupebit et natura
Cum resurget creatura
Judicanti responsura.

Liber scriptus proferetur
In quo totum continetur
Unde mundus judicetur.

Judex ergo cum sedebit
Quidquid latet apparebit
Nil inultum remanebit.

....

Lacrymosa dies illa,
Qua resurget ex favilla
Judicandus homo reus;

Huic ergo parce Deus:
Pie Jesu Domine,
Dona eis requiem.

[That day, the day of wrath, will turn the universe to ashes as David and the Sybil foretold.

A trumpet will scatter a marvellous sound throughout the earth's tombs and drive all souls before the throne.

Death and nature will be struck dumb when all creation rises to answer to the judge.

The written book in which all is recorded for the judgement of the world will be brought forth.

When the judge has taken his place all hidden things will be made manifest; no crime will remain unpunished.

Woeful will that day be when guilty man rises from the ashes to be judged.

Therefore, O God, spare mankind; sweet Jesus give them rest.]

A Lyke-Wake Dirge

Anon (16th century)

The progress of the human soul after death across the wildest part of
Yorkshire

This ae nighte, this ae nighte,
   Every nighte and alle,
Fire, and sleet, and candle-lighte;
   And Christe receive thye saule.

When thou from hence away art paste,
Every nighte and alle,
To Whinny-muir thou comest at laste;
   And Christe receive thye saule.

If ever thou gave hosen and shoon,
   Every nighte and alle,
Sot thee down and put them on;
   And Christe receive thye saule.

If hosen and shoon thou never gavest nane,
   Every nighte and alle,
The whinnes shall pinch thee to the bare bane
   And Christe receive thye saule.

From Whinny-muir when thou mayst passe,
   Every nighte and alle,
To Brig o' Dread thou comest at laste;
   And Christe receive thye saule.

From Brig o' Dread when thou mayst passe,
   Every nighte and alle,
To Purgatory fire thou comest at laste;
   And Christe receive thye saule.

If ever thou gavest meate and drinke,
    Every nighte and alle,
The fire shall never make thee shrinke;
    And Christe receive thye saule.

If meate or drinke thou gavest nane,
    Every nighte and alle,
The fire will burn thee to the bare bane;
    And Christe receive thye saule.

This ae nighte, this ae nighte,
    Every nighte and alle,
Fire, and sleet, and candle-lighte;
    And Christe receive thye saule.

'That Time of Year . . .'

William Shakespeare (1564–1616)

Sonnet LXXIII

That time of year thou mayst in me behold
When yellow leaves, or none, or few do hang
Upon those boughs which shake against the cold,
Bare ruined choirs where late the sweet birds sang.
In me thou see'st the twilight of such day
As after sunset fadeth in the west,
Which by and by black night doth take away,
Death's second self, that seals up all the rest.
In me thou see'st the glowing of such fire
That on the ashes of his youth doth lie,
As the deathbed whereon it must expire,
Consumed with that which it was nourished by.
    This thou perceiv'st, which makes thy love more
        strong,
    To love that well which thou must leave ere long.

'Fear No More the Heat o' the Sun'

William Shakespeare (1564–1616)

From *Cymbeline* (1610)

Fear no more the heat o' the sun
   Nor the furious winter's rages
Thou thy worldly task has done,
   Home art gone and ta'en thy wages:
Golden lads and girls all must,
Like chimney sweepers, come to dust.

Fear no more the frown o' the great
   Thou art past the tyrant's stroke;
Care no more to clothe and eat;
   To thee the reed is as the oak:
The sceptre, learning, physic must
All follow this and come to dust.

Fear no more the lightning-flash
   Nor the dreaded thunder-stone;
Fear nor slander, censure rash;
   Thou has finish'd joy and moan:
All lovers young, all lovers must
Consign to thee and come to dust.

No exorciser harm thee!
   Nor no witchcraft craft thee!
Ghost unlaid forbear thee!
   Nothing ill come near thee!
Quiet consummation have;
And renowned be thy grave.

'Aye, But to Die'

William Shakespeare (1564–1616)

From *Measure for Measure* (1604)

Aye, but to die, and go we know not where:
To lie in cold obstruction and to rot;
This sensible warm motion to become
A kneaded clod; and the delighted spirit
To bathe in fiery floods, or to reside
In thrilling region of thick-ribbèd ice;
To be imprison'd in the viewless winds,
And blown with restless violence round about
The pendent world; or to be worse than worst
Of those that lawless and incertain thoughts
Imagine howling: 'tis too horrible!
The weariest and most loathèd worldly life
That age, ache, penury and imprisonment
Can lay on nature is a paradise
To what we fear of death.

The Poet's Own Death

Thomas Gray (1716–71)

From 'Elegy Written in a Country Churchyard' (1751)

For thee who mindful of th' unhonoured dead,
   Dost in these lines their artless tale relate;
If chance, by lonely contemplation led,
   Some kindred spirit shall inquire thy fate,

Haply some hoary-headed swain may say,
　'Oft have we seen him at the peep of dawn
With eager steps brushing the dew away,
　To meet the sun upon the upland lawn;

'There at the foot of yonder nodding beech
　That wreathes its old fantastic roots so high,
His listless length at noontide he would stretch,
　And pore upon the brook that babbles by.

'Hard by yon wood, now smiling as in scorn
　Muttering his wayward fancies he would rove
Now drooping, woeful, wan like one forlorn,
　Or crazed with care, or cross'd in hopeless love.

'One morn I miss'd him on the custom'd hill
　Along the heath, or near his favourite tree;
Another came, nor yet beside the rill
　Nor up the lawn, nor at the wood was he.

'The next with dirges due in sad array
　Along the church-way path we saw him borne, –
Approach and read (for thou canst read) the lay
　Graved on the stone beneath that ancient thorn.'

The Epitaph

Here rests his head upon a lap of Earth
　A Youth to Fortune and to Fame unknown;
Fair Science frown'd not on his humble birth,
　And Melancholy mark'd him for her own.

Large was his bounty and his soul sincere,
　Heaven did a recompense as largely send:
He gave to Misery all he had, a tear,
He gained from Heaven 'twas all he wish'd a friend.

No farther seek his merits to disclose,
Or draw his frailties from their dread abode
(There they alike in trembling hope repose,)
The bosom of his Father and his God.

'At the Mid Hour of Night'

Thomas Moore (1779–1852)

At the mid hour of night, when stars are weeping, I fly
To the lone vale we loved, when life shone warm in
     thine eye;
And I think that, if spirits can steal from the regions
     of air
To revisit past scenes of delight, thou will come to me
     there,
And tell me our love is remembered even in the sky.

Then I sing the wild song it once was such rapture to
     hear,
When our voices commingling breathed like one on the
     ear;
And as Echo far off through the vale my sad orison
     rolls,
I think, O my love! 'tis thy voice from the Kingdom of
     Souls
Faintly answering still the notes that once were so dear.

A Winter's Night

William Barnes (1801–86)

It was a chilly winter's night;
   And frost was glittering on the ground,
And evening stars were twinkling bright;
   And from the gloomy plain around
     Came no sound,
But where, within the wood-girt tower,
The church bell slowly struck the hour

As if that all of human birth
   Had risen to the final day,
And soaring from the wornout earth
   Were called in hurry and dismay,
     Far away;
And I alone of all mankind
Were left in loneliness behind.

Edgar Allan Poe (1809–49)

It was many and many a year ago
    In a kingdom by the sea,
That a maiden there lived whom you may know
    By the name of Annabel Lee; –
And this maiden she lived with no other thought
    Than to love and be loved by me.

She was a child and I was a child,
    In this kingdom by the sea,
But we loved with a love that was more than love –
    I and my Annabel Lee –
With a love that the wingèd seraphs of Heaven
    Coveted her and me.

And this was the reason that, long ago,
    In the kingdom by the sea,
The wind blew out of a cloud by night
    Chilling my Annabel Lee;
So that her highborn kinsmen came
    And bore her away from me,
To shut her up in a sepulchre
    In this kingdom by the sea.

The angels, not half so happy in Heaven,
    Went envying her and me:–
Yes! that was the reason (as all the men know,
    In this kingdom by the sea)
That the wind came out of the cloud, chilling
    And killing my Annabel Lee.

But our love it was stronger by far than the love
    Of those who were older than we –
    Of many far wiser than we –
And neither the angels in Heaven above
    Nor the demons down under the sea,
Can ever dissever my soul from the soul
    Of the beautiful Annabel Lee: –

For the moon never beams without bringing me dreams
    Of the beautiful Annabel Lee;
And the stars never rise but I see the bright eyes
    Of the beautiful Annabel Lee;
And so, all the night-tide, I lie down by the side,
Of my darling, my darling, my life and my bride
    In her sepulchre there by the sea –
    In her tomb by the side of the sea.

[from] Ulysses

Alfred Lord Tennyson (1809–1892)

There lies the port; the vessel puffs her sail:
There gloom the dark, broad seas. My mariners,
Souls that have toiled, and wrought, and thought with
    me –
That ever with a frolic welcome took
The thunder and the sunshine, and opposed
Free hearts, free foreheads – you and I are old;
Old age hath yet his honour and his toil.
Death closes all; but something ere the end,
Some work of noble note, may yet be done,
Not unbecoming men that strove with Gods.
The lights begin to twinkle from the rocks:
The long day wanes; the slow moon climbs; the deep
Moans round with many voices. Come, my friends,
'Tis not too late to seek a newer world.
Push off and sitting well in order smite
The sounding furrows; for my purpose holds
To sail beyond the sunset, and the baths
Of all the western stars until I die.
It may be that the gulfs will wash us down;
It may be we shall touch the Happy Isles,
And see the great Achilles, whom we knew.
Though much is taken, much abides; and though
We are not now that strength which in old days
Moved earth and heaven; that which we are, we are;
One equal temper of heroic hearts,
Made weak by time and fate, but strong in will
To strive, to seek, to find, and not to yield.

[from] Tithonus

Alfred Lord Tennyson (1809–1892)

The woods decay, the woods decay and fall,
The vapours weep their burthen to the ground,
Man comes and tills the fields and lies beneath,
And after many a summer dies the swan.
Me only cruel immortality
Consumes: I wither slowly in thine arms,
Here at the quiet limit of the world,
A white-haired shadow roaming like a dream
The ever-silent spaces of the East,
Far-folded mists, and gleaming halls of morn.

....

   Yet hold me not for ever in thine East:
How can my nature longer mix with thine?
Coldly thy rosy shadows bathe me, cold
Are all thy lights, and cold my wrinkled feet
Upon thy glimmering thresholds, when the stream
Floats up from those dim fields about the homes
Of happy men that have the power to die,
And grassy barrows of the happier dead,
Release me, and restore me to the ground.
Thou seëst all things, thou wilt see my grave:
Thou wilt renew thy beauty morn by morn;
I earth in earth forget these empty courts,
And thee returning on thy silver wheels.

[In Greek mythology Tithonus was a beautiful youth beloved of Eos,
the goddess of the dawn, who asked Zeus to grant him immortality
but neglected to ask for eternal youth. He gradually became unnaturally
old and in mercy Eos turned him into a cicada which sloughs its aged
skin every year.]

Crossing the Bar

Alfred Lord Tennyson (1809–1892)

Sunset and evening star,
    And one clear call for me.
And may there be no moaning of the bar,
    When I put out to sea.

But such a tide as moving seems asleep
    Too full for sound and foam,
When that which drew from out the boundless deep
Turns again home.

Twilight and evening bell
    And after that the dark;
And may there be no sadness of farewell,
    When I embark!

For tho' from out our bourne of Time and place
    The flood may bear me far,
I hope to see my Pilot face to face,
    When I have crost the bar.

Prospice

Robert Browning (1812–1989)

Written in 1864, three years after the death of his wife

Fear death? – to feel the fog in my throat,
    The mist in my face,
When the snows begin, and the blasts denote
    I am nearing the place,
The power of the night, the press of the storm,
    The post of the foe;
Where he stands, the arch fear in a visible form,
    Yet the strong man must go:
For the journey is done and the summit attained,
    And the barriers fall,
Though a battle's to fight ere the guerdon be gained,
    The reward of it all.
I was ever a fighter, so – one fight more,
    The best and the last!
I would hate that death bandaged my eyes, and
      forbore,
    And bade me creep past.
No! let me taste the whole of it, fare like my peers
    The heroes of old,
Bear the brunt and in a minute pay glad life's arrears
    Of pain, darkness and cold.
For sudden the worst turns the best to the brave,
    The black minute's at end,
And the element's rage, the fiend-voices that rave,
    Shall dwindle, shall blend,
Shall change, shall become first a peace out of pain,
    Then a light, then thy breast,
O thou soul of my soul! I shall claps thee again,
And with God be the rest!

prospice = look forward; guerdon = reward

Heraclitus

W[illiam] J[ohnson] Cory (1823–92)

Version of an epigram by an assistant master at Eton (1845–72) from
the Greek of Callimachus (*c.* 310–*c.* 240) which was written for a friend
from Halicarnassus in Caria in Asia Minor.

They told me, Heraclitus, they told me you were dead;
They brought me bitter news to hear and bitter tears
     to shed.
I wept as I remembered how often you and I
Had tired the sun with talking and sent him down the
     sky.

And now that thou art lying, my dear old Carian guest
A handful of grey ashes, long long ago at rest,
Still are thy pleasant voice, thy nightingales, awake,
For Death, he taketh all away, but them he cannot
     take.

Because I Could Not Stop for Death

Emily Dickinson (1830–86)

Because I could not stop for Death –
He kindly stopped for me –
The Carriage held but just Ourselves –
And Immortality.

We slowly drove – He knew no haste
And I had put away
My labor and my leisure too,
For his Civility –

We passed the School, where Children strove
At Recess – in the Ring –
We passed the Fields of Gazing Grain –
We passed the Setting Sun –

Or rather – He passed Us –
The Dews drew quivering and chill –
For only Gossamer my Gown –
My Tippet – only Tulle –

We paused before a House that seemed
A Swelling of the Ground –
The Roof was scarcely visible –
The Cornice – in the Ground –

Since then - 'tis Centuries – and yet
Feels shorter than the Day
I first surmised the Horses Heads
Were toward Eternity –

Song

Christina Rossetti (1830–94)

When I am dead, my dearest,
    Sing no sad songs for me;
Plant thou no roses at my head,
    Nor shady cypress tree:
Be the green grass above me
    With showers and dewdrops wet;
And if thou wilt, remember,
And if thou wilt, forget.

I shall not see the shadows,
    I shall not feel the rain;
I shall not hear the nightingale
    Sing on, as if in pain;
And dreaming through the twilight
    That doth not rise nor set,
Haply I may remember,
    And haply may forget.

The Dead

Rupert Brooke (1887–1915)

Written in 1914 just after Brooke's joining of the Royal Naval Division

These hearts were woven of human joys and cares,
    Washed marvellously with sorrow, swift to mirth.
The years had given them kindness. Dawn was theirs,
    And sunset and the colours of the earth.
These had seen movement and heard music; known
    Slumber and waking; loved; gone proudly friended;
Felt the quick stir of wonder; sat alone;
    Touched flowers and furs and cheeks. All this is
        ended.

There are waters blown by changing winds to laughter
And lit by the rich skies all day. And after,
    Frost with a gesture, stays the waves that dance
And wandering loveliness. He leaves a white
    Unbroken glory. a gathered radiance,
A width, a shining peace, under the night.

Rendezvous

Alan Seeger (1888–1917)

I have a rendezvous with Death
At some disputed barricade,
When Spring comes back with rustling shade
And apple-blossom fills the air –
I have a rendezvous with Death
When Spring brings back blue days and fair.

It may be he shall take my hand
And lead me into his dark land
And close my eyes and quench my breath –
It may be I shall pass him still.
I have a rendezvous with Death
On some scarred slope of battered hill.
When Spring comes round again this year
And the first meadow-flowers appear.

God knows 'twere better to be deep
Pillowed in silk and scented down,
Where loves throbs out in blissful sleep,
Pulse nigh to pulse, and breath to breath,
Where hushed awakenings are dear . . .
But I've a rendezvous with Death
At midnight in some flaming town
When Spring trips north again this year,
And to my pledged word am true,
I shall not fail my rendezvous.

Anthem for Doomed Youth

Wilfred Owen (1893–1918)

What passing-bells for these who die as cattle?
    Only the monstrous anger of the guns.
    Only the stuttering rifles' rapid rattle
Can patter out their hasty orisons.
No mockeries for them for prayers or bells,
    Nor any voice of mourning save the choirs –
The shrill, demented choirs of wailing shells;
    And bugles calling for them from sad shires.

What candles may be held to speed them all?
    Not in the hands of boys, but in their eyes
Shall shine the holy glimmers of goodbyes.
    The pallor of girls' brows shall be their pall;
Their flowers the tenderness of silent minds,
And each slow dusk a drawing-down of blinds.

Biographical Index

William Allingham was born in Ballyshannon, County Donegal in 1824, and served as a customs officer all over Ulster. He was a disciple of Tennyson and became a fringe member of the Pre-Raphaelite Brotherhood when he was happily transferred to the English collection. Some of his poems remain favourites but his novel in verse *Laurence Bloomfield in Ireland* (1864) is his finest work. He died in 1869 and is buried in Ballyshannon.

The Arch-poet is the author of ten elegantly rowdy twelfth-century poems. Of Germanic origin, he died *c.* 1165.

St Thomas Aquinas was born of an aristocratic family in Aquino, Italy in 1225 and educated by the Benedictines and at the University of Naples. He became a Dominican in spite of fierce family opposition including house arrest. His *Summa Theologica* (1266–73) which earned him the honour *Doctor Angelicus* still largely represents Catholic theological teaching. He died in Fossanuova in 1274 and was canonised in 1323.

Matthew Arnold was born near Staines in Middlesex in 1822 and educated at his father's school, Rugby, and Balliol College, Oxford. He was appointed a school inspector in 1851 and during his thirty-five years' service brought about much educational reform. His poetry was popular and he saw himself as leading the attack on contemporary philistinism. He was appointed professor of poetry at Oxford in 1857 and wrote much critical and philosophical prose before his death in 1888.

William Blake was born in London in 1757, the son of an Irish hosier, and became an engraver. His visions drove him to write mystic poetry which he engraved with accompanying illustrations on copper. His *Illustrations to the Book of Job*, done when he was seventy, show remarkable artistic talent and visionary insight. He died in 1827.

Riocard Bairéid was born near Erris, County Mayo *c.* 1740 and spent the rest of his life there as teacher and small farmer. He was a witty and vigorous raconteur, in great demand as an entertainer for the local gentry. He died in 1819.

William Barnes was born near Sturminster-Newtown in Dorset in 1800. After some years as a clerk and teacher he went to St John's, Cambridge and took holy orders. He was appointed to parishes in his native county and became widely known for his poems in the often dense Dorset dialect, 'the bold and broad Doric of England'. He died in 1886.

Nicholas Breton was born in London *c.* 1545 and educated at Oxford. He was a prolific writer of prose, verse and pamphlets, his best known poetic work being *The Passionate Shepheard* (1604) and a book on angling which anticipated the work of Izaak Walton. He died *c.* 1626.

Elizabeth Barrett Browning was born in Durham in 1806 and, after a period as a semi-invalid in her family house in Wimpole Street, London, married Robert Browning against strong and morbid paternal opposition. She lived happily and healthily in Pisa and Florence until her death in 1861.

Robert Browning was born in Camberwell, London, in 1812, the son of a bank official. He married Elizabeth Barrett, who was six years his senior, in 1846, and lived with her in Italy until her death in 1861. He returned to England with his son, having written brilliant long poems and vigorous novels in verse. He died in 1889.

Robert Burns was born in Alloway, Ayrshire in 1759. He was for the time and place well educated and far from the 'illiterate plowboy genius' his Edinburgh patrons preferred to regard him. His amorous and bibulous career was not abnormal for the period and his poetic talent, especially in writing love songs, his humour and egalitarianism have gained him lasting popularity. He died of overwork and fever in 1796.

George Gordon, Lord Byron was born London of Scots ancestry in 1788 and educated at Harrow and Trinity College, Cambridge where in spite of a club-foot he excelled at sport and venery. He succeeded to the title in 1798 but his childhood was miserable, having to put up with the rage and misery of a deserted and bankrupt mother. He wrote extended satirical and romantic poetry which gave the world the epithet 'Byronic' and from an early age was 'mad, bad and dangerous to know', being accused of incest with his half-sister. More Augustan in his poetry than his slightly younger Romantic peers, his poetry, especially *English Bards and Scottish Reviewers* (1809), *Childe Harold's Pilgrimage* (1812) and *Don Juan* (1824) is still deservedly popular. His reputation was restored by his active involvement in the Greek War of Independence, and after his death at Missolonghi in 1824 he was brought home to a hero's funeral.

Charles Stuart Calverley was born in Worcestershire in 1831, the son of a country parson, and educated at Harrow, Oxford and Cambridge, becoming a fellow of Christ's College, Cambridge in 1858. He was called to the bar in London in 1865. A brilliant career as an advocate ended in a skating accident in 1866 and he was an invalid for the rest of his life. Though an effective lyric poet it is his talent as a humorist and parodist that has made his verse still readable today. He died in 1884.

Henry Carey was born in Yorkshire *c.* 1690 and wrote many songs and theatrical burlesques for which he also provided the music. As well as the famous 'Sally in Our Alley' he is credited with some of the verses of 'God Save the King'. He died in 1743.

Seathrún Céitinn (aka Geoffrey Keating) was born *c.* 1570 in Tipperary of Norman–Irish stock and educated for the priesthood in Bordeaux, returning to Ireland in 1610 a DD. As a parish priest of Tubrid near his birthplace he was critical of the morals of local squireens and had to go into hiding. The legend is that his great work of historiography *Foras Feasa ar Éirinn* (completed 1640) was finished in a cave. The details of his death are obscure but it probably occurred in his living of Cappoquin *c.* 1645.

Thomas of Celano was born in Celano in the Abruzzi and became an early follower of St Francis of Assisi, whose biographer he became. He is taken to be the author of *Dies Irae*. He died *c.* 1255.

Geoffrey Chaucer was born in London *c.* 1345, the son of a vintner and tavern keeper. He became a page at the court of Edward III and eventually head of the customs service. His chief works are *Troilus and Criseyde* (1385) and *The Canterbury Tales* (begun 1387). He died in 1400 and was buried in Westminster Abbey in the part that has since become known as Poets' Corner.

Arthur Hugh Clough was born in Liverpool in 1810, the son of a Liverpool cotton merchant who emigrated to Charleston in 1823. The boy became one of Rugby's brightest stars and he became a close friend of Matthew Arnold, the headmaster's son who commemorated him in his poem 'Thyrsis'. Deeply concerned with matters of faith, he nearly followed Newman into the Catholic Church but remained a sceptic. He died in 1861 a noted republican.

Samuel Taylor Coleridge was born in 1772 in Ottery St Mary, Devonshire, where his father was vicar, and was educated at Christ's Hospital, London where he first met his close friend Charles Lamb, who later described him as 'an archangel, slightly damaged'. He was an editor, Unitarian minister, poet and chronic sufferer from toothache and neuralgia, a condition that led to his being addicted to opium. A brilliant interpreter of Shakespeare, he was one of the founders of the Romantic Movement. He spent the last twenty years of his life in the homes of various friends, including the Wordsworths. He died in his sleep in a friend's house in Highgate in 1834.

William Johnson Cory was born in Torrington, Devonshire in 1823 and educated at Eton and King's College, Cambridge. He taught at his old school for twenty-six years, writing for it the 'Eton Boating Song' which was published in 1863. He inherited an estate in 1872, on the condition that he add Cory to his birthname, and lived in Hampstead until his death in 1892.

Abraham Cowley was born in 1618 in London, the posthumous son of a stationer, and educated at Westminster and Trinity College, Cambridge. A vociferous Royalist, he was expelled from parliamentary Cambridge in 1644 but continued his education at Oxford. He continued to support the queen after Charles I's death and, after some bleak years during the Protectorate, was granted a comfortable provision at the time of the Restoration. He died in 1687.

Richard Crashaw was born *c.* 1612 in London, the son of a Puritan clergyman. He was educated at Charterhouse and Pembroke Hall, Cambridge, becoming a fellow of Peterhouse *c.* 1636. He moved from Puritanism to Anglicanism and by 1645 was a Catholic exile in Paris. Famous for his religious poetry, his later poverty was ameliorated by appointment as a subcanon of Loreto in April 1649, but he died four months later.

John Philpot Curran was born in Newmarket, County Cork in 1750 and after education at TCD and the Middle Temple, London, was called to the Irish bar in 1775. He entered the Irish parliament in 1783 and had a somewhat turbulent career, fighting in five duels. He was pro-Catholic and anti-Union and spent his last years in London in the congenial company of Moore, Sheridan and Byron, dying in Brompton in 1817.

Thomas Dekker was born *c.* 1572 in London, a city that figures in his pamphlets and his most famous play *The Shoemakers Holiday* (1600). He had contemporary fame as a prose satirist, being known especially for *The Gull's Hornbook* (1609). He died in 1632.

Emily Dickinson was born in 1830 and lived all her life in the family home at Amherst, Massachusetts. Well-educated, she withdrew from public life in 1853 and lived in seclusion, writing many poems and dressing entirely in white, a habit that earned her the soubriquet the Nun of Amherst. She died in 1886.

John Donne was born in London in 1572 and brought up as a Catholic, a faith he relinquished to become in time a distinguished Anglican Dean of St Paul's, famous for the excellence of his sermons. His poetry is difficult but elegantly wrought and is much more popular in modern times than it was at his death in 1631.

Michael Drayton was born, like Shakespeare, in Warwickshire, and in the same year, 1564. He spent his life in the households of wealthy patrons and tradition has it that it was after a bout of drinking with him and Ben Jonson that the ailing Shakespeare was taken ill and died. His best known poem 'Fair Stood the Wind for France' describes Henry V's success at Agincourt. He died in 1631 and is buried in Poets' Corner.

Ernest Dowson was born in Kent in 1867 and spent much of his youth and later life in France. He left Queen's College, Oxford without taking a degree, to manage his father's dry dock. His 'decadent' poems were largely inspired by his obsession with 'Cynara', the daughter of an Italian café owner who afterwards married a waiter. Both his parents were tubercular and committed suicide and Ernest, who inherited the condition, aggravated it with chronic alcoholism. He became a Catholic, as was the fashion, and died in France in 1900.

William Dunbar was born *c.* 1460 in East Lothian. After study at St Andrews he became a Franciscan friar but later left the order to become a diplomat for James IV. He was part of the embassy that arranged the king's marriage with Margaret Tudor and composed his most famous work *The Thissil and the Rois* (1503) in her honour. He died *c.* 1510.

Edward Fitzgerald was born in Suffolk in 1809 and educated there and at Trinity College, Cambridge. A friend of Tennyson, he stayed in Suffolk all his life, without profession except as an unpaid deckhand with the fishermen of Lowestoft. He has everlasting fame for his version of the quatrains of Omar Khayyhám and was treasured by a wide circle of correspondents for his excellent letters. He died in 1893.

Thomas Flatman was born in London in 1637 and educated at Winchester and New College, Oxford. Known equally as a miniaturist and poet, he published *Poems and Songs* (1674) and died in 1688.

James Elroy Flecker was born in Lewisham in South London in 1884 and studied oriental languages at Trinity College, Cambridge before joining the consular service. In 1910 he was posted to Constantinople where he met his Greek wife Hella Skiardessi. He was vice-consul in Beirut from 1911 until 1913 when his health broke down and he died in a sanatorium in Davos in 1915. His fascination with the Middle East began when he stole his first copy of Fitzgerald's *Rubá'iyát* and all his poetry and his exotic play *Hassan* (first produced in 1922) reflect this attraction.

Percy French was born in Clooneyquin, County Roscommon in 1854 and after a leisurely student career at Trinity eventually became an engineer in County Cavan. Already author of such comic songs as 'Abdul the Bulbul Ameer' he became a full-time comic entertainer on the death of his wife, travelling round Ireland with a show based on his own material, which included such songs as 'The Mountains of Mourne' and 'Come Back, Paddy Reilly', and also featured his talents as a lightning water-colourist. He died in Formby, Lancashire in 1920.

Oliver Goldsmith, born in Lissoy, County Westmeath was the son of the local curate, who was the model for his popular novel *The Vicar of Wakefield* (1764). He graduated from TCD after s ome interruptions and later appeared in London claiming a medical degree from Leyden. A member of Dr Johnson's 'club', he supported himself as a literary hack but managed to write one of the most popular poems - *The Deserted Village* (1770) - and one of the finest comedies - *She Stoops to Conquer* (1773) - in the English language. He died of the fever in 1774.

Eva Gore-Booth, the sister of the revolutionary Countess Markievicz, was born in the family home at Lissadell in County Sligo in 1870. She moved to Manchester with her partner Esther Roper in 1892 and began a lifetime commitment to feminism and pacificism. She wrote much poetry and unstageable drama and died in Hampstead in 1926.

Thomas Grey was born in London in 1716 and educated at Eton, the subject of one of his famous poems, and Peterhouse, Cambridge, where he became professor of Modern History in 1768. World famous as the author of the 'Elegy', he was buried in the country churchyard of Stoke Poges in 1771.

Thomas Hardy was born in Dorset, the 'Wessex' of his many novels in 1840 and trained as an architect. In his thirties he began to write novels which increased in excellence and frankness until *Tess of the D'Urbervilles* (1891) and *Jude the Obscure* (1895) proved too strong for the late Victorian public and he gave up fiction in disgust. He continued to write poetry, however, and was awarded the OM in 1910 eighteen years before his death.

William Ernest Henley was born in Gloucester in 1848, the son of bookseller. He contracted tuberculosis as a child, losing a foot and spending two years in Edinburgh Infirmary (1873–5) receiving successful treatment to save the other. His poems written there won him the friendship of Robert Louis Stevenson who used him as the inspiration for his great piratical sea-cook Long John Silver. He was an energetic editor, a compiler of a dictionary of slang and an unabashed happy imperialist who wrote inspirational verse for young Britons. He died in 1903.

Robert Herrick was born in 1591, the son of a London goldsmith. He went to Cambridge and became vicar of Dean Prior in Devon in 1629. Because of assumed parliamentary support he lost his living at the Restoration. He died in 1674, famous for his lyrics on love and the countryside.

James Hogg, known in his lifetime as the 'Ettrick Shepherd' was born in Ettrick Forest, Selkirkshire in 1770. Like Burns his ballads and songs made him an accepted figure in Edinburgh society. He also wrote a prose classic of the macabre, *Private Memoirs and Confessions of a Justified Sinner* (1824). He died in Edinburgh in 1835.

Gerard Manley Hopkins was born in Stratford, Essex (now part of Greater London) in 1844 and as an undergraduate at Balliol College, Oxford, came under the influence of Newman. He became a Catholic and was ordained a Jesuit priest in 1877, symbolically burning his poems but prudently sending copies to his friend the poet Robert Bridges. He was appointed to the chair of Greek at the Royal University in Dublin in 1884 and died there of typhoid in 1899.

Leigh Hunt was born in 1784 in Southgate, Middlesex and was educated at Christ's Hospital, afterwards becoming a radical journalist. He was imprisoned for two years (1813–15) for a libel on the Prince Regent. He was the first publisher of Shelley and Keats, and a close friend of Byron. He tended to be kindly but feckless and his many children ran wild, usually in other people's houses. He outlived most of his more talented and famous contemporaries, dying in 1859.

Ben Jonson was born in Westminster in 1572, the posthumous son of a Border clergyman. He was educated at Westminster and led the uneasy literary life of the period, acting, working as a bricklayer and writing great comedies, notably *Volpone* (1601), *The Alchemist* (1610) and *Bartholomew Fair* (1615). His quarrelsome nature led to his killing at least one man and serving time in gaol. His lyrics are second only to Shakspeare's. He died in 1637 after establishing a considerable reputation as a writer of masques.

John Keats was born in London in 1795 and qualified as a surgeon in Guy's Hospital. He published his first book *Poems* in 1811, by then already ill with tuberculosis. Later work was savaged by critics who found his heady sensuousness unnerving. He made a painful journey to Italy on Shelley's invitation in the autumn of 1824 but died the following February.

Charles Kingsley was born a vicar's son in Dartmoor in 1819. He was educated at King's College, London and Magdalene College, Cambridge, taking orders in 1846 and was appointed rector at Eversley, Hampshire, where he lived for the rest of his life. He was known for his 'muscular Christianity', a description he deprecated, and though famous as the author of such exciting historical romances as *Westward Ho!* (1855) and the socially conscious *The Water Babies* (1863) was also known for his anti-Catholicism and attacks on Newman. He had several nervous breakdowns and died, comparatively young, in 1875.

Walter Savage Landor was born in Warwick in 1775, the son of a doctor. He was expelled from both Rugby and Trinity College, Oxford, rowed with his father and lived for the rest of his quarrelsome life on an allowance supplemented by earnings from writing, notably his prose masterpiece, *Imaginary Conversations* (1824–9). He died in Florence in 1864.

William Larminie was born in Castlebar, County Mayo, in 1849 and educated at TCD before serving in the India Office in London. Regarded as a forerunner of the Irish Renaissance, his work was greatly admired by Yeats. His poetry reflects his interest in Irish folklore and its assonance is a tribute to Gaelic verse of which he had some knowledge. Among his philosophical works is a translation of Eriugena's *Peri Phuseon*. He died in Bray in 1900.

Francis Ledwidge was born in Slane, County Meath, the son of an evicted farmer. Having read his early poems the local landlord Lord Dunsany encouraged him to write – and to join the British army at the outbreak of war in 1914. He survived the Gallipoli landings but was killed in Belgium in 1917.

Henry Wadsworth Longfellow was born in Portland, Maine in 1807 and graduated from Bowdoin College in that state. He held the chair of foreign languages in his alma mater and later became professor of modern languages and literature at Harvard. He is now remembered mainly for some ballads, especially 'Paul Revere's Ride' (1863), and 'Hiawatha' (1855) which retells Amerindian legends in insistent metre. He died in 1882.

Richard Lovelace was born in Woolwich in 1618 and educated at Charterhouse and Gloucester Hall, Oxford. He became a courtier and loyal supporter of Charles I, and was deep in anti-Parliamentary activity well before the Civil War. He beggared himself in the cause and died in poverty in 1657, having spent some time in the service of Louis XIV of France.

Thomas MacDonagh was born in Cloughjordan, County Tipperary in 1878 and educated at the Royal University, the staff of which he joined (as UCD) in 1912 after working with Pearse in St Enda's. He was director of training for the Irish Volunteers and commander in Jacobs during the Easter Rising. He was executed with Pearse and Thomas Clarke on 3 May 1916.

Leonard McNally was born in 1752 in Dublin and educated at TCD. He wrote many comic operas and plays for the London stage. He was a government informer for the British authorities during the period of the United Irishmen, responsible for the taking of Lord Edward Fitzgerald, and as Emmet's counsel, revealing the case for the defence to the prosecution before the trial. He died in 1820.

Robert Mannyng, also known as Robert of Brunne, was born in Bourne in Lincolnshire. A Gilbertine monk, he is chiefly known as a chronicler and as the author of a moral manual, *Handlynge Synne* (*c.* 1303). He died *c.* 1338.

Andrew Marvell was born in Yorkshire in 1621 and educated at Trinity College, Cambridge. He became John Milton's assistant in Cromwell's government but had many Royalist friends, indicating his independence in his 'Horatian Ode upon Cromwell's Return from Ireland' which has a moving description of Charles I's execution. His poetry had to wait till modern times for wide appreciation. A friend of Charles II in spite of his republicanism, he died in 1678 as a result of medical incompetence.

James Clerk Maxwell was born in 1831 in Edinburgh, the son of a lawyer. He became one of the world's greatest theoretical physicists, paving the way for the work of Einstein and others. He died, Cavendish professor of experimental physics, at Cambridge in 1879.

Alice Meynell née Thompson was born in Barnes, London in 1847. She spent her childhood on the continent, becoming a Catholic in 1868. Her poems attracted the attention of Wilfred Meynell, whom she married in 1877. She died in 1922.

Richard Monckton-Milnes, Lord Houghton was born in 1809 and was an 'Apostle' at Cambridge and friend of Thackeray and Tennyson. He was MP for Pontefract from 1837 until 1863 when he entered the House of Lords. Known as an adventurous traveller and wit he devoted his life to liberal causes. He died in 1895.

John Milton was born in Cheapside in the city of London in 1608, the son of a composer, and led a life in which humanism and Puritanism struggled for mastery. After Shakespeare the greatest English poet, his classical training caused him to essay not only a Homeric epic, *Paradise Lost* (comp. 1664) but also a Sophoclean tragedy, *Samson Agonistes* (1671). He was Cromwell's Latin secretary during the Commonwealth and paid the penalty at the Restoration. He was soon pardoned by Charles II and though blind lived the last dozen years of his life in comfort, tended by his third wife, a woman forty years his junior. He died in 1674.

Clement Clarke Moore was born in New York in 1779 and taught Hebrew in the General Theological Seminary which he helped found. Famous as the author of 'The Night before Christmas' he is largely responsible for the present-day persona of Father Christmas. He died in Providence, Rhode Island in 1863.

Thomas Moore was born in Dublin in 1779 and educated in TCD. He moved to London where he became the darling of Whig drawing rooms, singing his own songs which he set to old Irish airs. He was a great ambassador for Ireland, friendly with Robert Emmet and regarded as a finer poet than his friend Byron. He died after a period of premature senility in Wiltshire in 1852.

Thomas Nashe was born in Lowestoft, the son of a clergyman and educated at St John's College, Cambridge. He lived mainly by writing often vituperative anti-Puritan pamphlets and was imprisoned in the Fleet for his play *The Isle of Dogs* (1597). He died in 1601 after completing the satirical masque *Summer's Last Will and Testament*.

John Henry Newman was born in London in 1801 and after a sternly religious upbringing went to Trinity College, Oxford, becoming a fellow of Oriel in 1822. The intellectual star of the Oxford Movement, his 'poping' in 1845 was one of the sensations of the century. He joined the order of the Oratory and after parish work in Edgbaston was invited by Archbishop Cullen to lead the Dublin Catholic University in 1854. His *Apologia pro*

Vita Sua (1864) was a riposte to Charles Kingsley's remark about Catholic truthfulness. He was made cardinal in 1879 and died in Edgbaston in 1890.

Antaine Ó Reachtabhra was born near Kiltimagh, in County Mayo about 1784. Blinded by smallpox at the age of nine, he became a travelling fiddler who entertained company in big house and tavern with his own songs and poems, which include his spring song '*Cill Aodáin*' and '*Eanach Dhúin*', the latter written as a lament for those drowned in the Corrib disaster of 1822. He died *c.* 1835.

Thomas William Hazen Rolleston was born in Shinrone, King's County in 1857 and educated at St Columba's and TCD. After four years in Germany (1879–83) he returned to Ireland and founded the *Dublin University Review*. He became interested in Gaelic literature and was an active if critical member of the Gaelic League. He died in his Hampstead home in 1920.

Arthur O'Shaughnessy was born in London of Irish parents in 1844. In 1861 he began work in the British Museum, moving to the natural history department in 1863. Like Allingham he was on the fringe of the Pre-Raphaelite movement, his famous poem 'Ode' having something of its colour and romantic detail. He died in 1881.

Wilfred Owen was born near Oswestry in Shropshire in 1893 and after being deprived of a university education because of lack of money taught English in the Berlitz school at Bordeaux in 1913. He enlisted in the army in 1915 and was wounded at the Somme. While convalescing at Craiglockart, he met Siegfried Sassoon, who encouraged him to continue with his poems. He was posted back to France and killed a week before the Armistice. He is regarded as the supreme Great War poet whose poetry told of 'War and the pity of War'.

George Peele was born in London and educated at Oxford. Returning to London he lived a rackety life (not unlike that of his contemporary Shakespeare) as actor, poet and playwright. His best known work is *The Old Wives Tale* (1595) written three years before his death in 1598.

James Payn was born in Cheltenham in 1830 and educated at Eton and Trinity College, Cambridge. He wrote a hundred novels including *The Luck of the Darrells* (1885) and was editor of both *Chamber's* and *Cornhill*. He died in 1898.

Padraic Pearse was born in Dublin in 1879 and educated at the Royal University, graduating as a barrister, though he rarely practised. His ideal of a free and Gaelic Ireland led to the founding of a school, St Enda's, where he put in practice his own much-considered views on education. He led the Easter Rising of 1916 and was executed on May 3.

Edgar Allan Poe was born in Virginia in 1809, the son of itinerant and short-lived actors. He was adopted by a long-suffering Virginia tobacco exporter, John Allan, whose name he incorporated in his own. His academic brilliance and pleasing personality fell victim to drink, gambling and drugs. He arranged to be expelled from the US military academy of West Point and lived by editing and writing poetry and some of the best Gothic tales and early detective fiction. In 1836 he married a thirteen-year-old cousin who died when she was twenty-four. His own wished-for death followed in 1849.

Alexander Pope was born in London in 1688. The son of a Catholic draper, his health was permanently affected by tuberculosis of the spine at the age of thirteen, leaving him a mere 4ft 6in in height. A brilliant poet and satirist, his personality was abrasive and unforgiving, though loved by such friends as Swift and for a time Lady Mary Wortley Montagu. He died in 1744.

Sir Walter Raleigh was born near Sidmouth in Devonshire in 1552. He left Oriel College to pursue a military career and in 1580 helped suppress the Desmond rising with notable savagery. He became a particular favourite with Elizabeth I who sent him to America where he named the colony of Virginia after her. Sentenced to perpetual imprisonment in the Tower at her death he wrote a *History of the World* (1614). He was released in 1616 to find gold for James I in the Orinoco but the expedition failed and he was beheaded in 1618.

John Wilmot, Earl of Rochester was born in 1647 in Ditchley, Oxfordshire and educated at Wadham College, Oxford. He showed great courage in the war with Holland in 1665 and, marrying an heiress, led the life of a Restoration rake. He wrote many excellently improper poems and satires. He died repentant in 1680.

Christina Rossetti was born in London in 1830, the sister of (and a much better poet than) Dante Gabriel, one the founders of the Pre-Raphaelite Brotherhood. She was three-quarters Italian and a fervent Anglican, dismissing a fiancé who had become a Catholic. She looked after her invalid mother who did not die until 1866, and thereafter led the life of a lay religious. She died in 1894, one of the finest poets in English.

Alan Seeger was born in New York in 1888 and educated at Harvard where he edited the *Harvard Monthly*. He made France his home and joined the Foreign Legion in 1914. He fought at the Somme in 1916 and was killed at Belloy-en-Santerre in 1917, being posthumously awarded the *Médaille Militaire* and the *Croix de Guerre*.

William Shakespeare was born in Stratford-on-Avon in 1564 and and left his wife Anne Hathaway, his senior by eight years, to work as an actor and dramatist in London. He wrote thirty-four plays between 1590 and 1612 and then retired to the life of a significant burgher of his native town. The supreme genius of English writers, parts of his life remain shrouded and his authorship of the works has often been vainly challenged. He died in Stratford in 1616.

Percy Bysshe Shelley was born in Sussex in 1792 and educated at Eton and University College, Cambridge. Sent down in 1811 for publishing a pamphlet on atheism, he married the sixteen-year-old Harriet Westbrooke against the wishes of both fathers who afterwards relented. He eloped with Mary Godwin in 1814 and married her when Harriet drowned herself in the Serpentine. They moved to Italy, gathering round them a coterie of artists and poets which included Byron. He was accidentally drowned near Lerici in 1822 and was buried in Rome near the grave of his younger friend Keats.

Robert Southwell was born probably in 1561 in Horsham, Norwich. Educated at Douai and Rome he became a Jesuit in 1578 and was ordained in 1584, coming to England two years later. He was betrayed to the authorities in 1592 and hanged and quartered at Tyburn in 1595. He was beatified by Pius XI in 1929.

Edmund Spenser was born in London *c.* 1552 and educated at Pembroke Hall, Cambridge. He became a courtier on the strength of *The Shepheard's Calendar* (1579) and went as secretary to Lord Grey de Wilton on his successful mission to crush the Desmond revolt in Munster. He was rewarded with Kilcolman Castle in County Cork where he lived with interruptions from 1586 until 1598, writing *The Faerie Queen* (1590) and *Colin Clout's Come Home Again* (1595). In 1598 he was burned out of his 'undertaking' by the revolting Irish and died in London the following year.

Robert Louis Stevenson was born in Edinburgh in 1850, the descendant of several generations of lighthouse engineers. Chronic ill health prevented his following the family profession and after qualifying as an advocate in 1875, he left home to travel in search of health and adventure. He was fascinated by his native city's combination of Calvinism and vice, which gave him the theme for his famous *Dr Jekyll and Mr Hyde* (1886) and *The Master of Ballantrae* (1889) and he wrote brilliantly for children both in prose – *Treasure Island* (1883) and *Kidnapped* (1886) – and verse – *A Child's Garden of Verses* (1885). As well as the author of novels and short stories he was a brilliant travel writer and essayist. He died in Vailima, Samoa, where he had set up a ménage with his wife, the divorcée Fanny Osbourne.

Sir John Suckling was born of a strongly Royalist family in Norfolk in 1609 and educated at Trinity College, Cambridge. He inherited large estates and was knighted in 1630. A noted gambler, he is said to have invented the card game of cribbage. He tried to rescue Charles I's favourite Strafford from the Tower and, having failed, fled to the continent, where he is believed to have committed suicide by poison in 1642.

Jonathan Swift, the greatest of Irish satirists, was born in Dublin in 1667 and educated at Kilkenny and TCD, afterwards taking holy orders. He was appointed secretary to Sir William Temple at Moor Park, near Rickmansworth in Hertfordshire, where he met Hester Johnston, the 'Stella' of his protracted love affair. Blocked from preferment by Queen Anne, who found *A Tale of A Tub* (1704) irreligious, he was appointed Dean of St Patrick's in Dublin, which he regarded as a sentence of actual and intellectual exile. His time in the city (1713–45) apart from the last three 'twilight' years was spent in the service on Dublin's poor and in active opposition to English malpractice in Ireland. He died in 1745 and was buried beside Stella in St Patrick's.

Alfred Tennyson (ennobled in 1884) was born in Somersby, Lincolnshire in 1809, the son of the rector. The early death in 1833 of his friend Arthur Hallam whom he met at Trinity College, Cambridge had a profound effect upon him, and his finest poetic work, *In Memoriam* (1850), was written in dedication. He succeeded Wordsworth as Poet Laureate in 1850 and by the time of his death in 1892 was a national institution.

William Makepeace Thackeray was born in 1811 in Calcutta, where his father worked for the East India Company. His father died in 1816 and after his mother's remarriage he was sent home. He was educated at Charterhouse and Trinity College, Cambridge, but left without taking a degree. He spent his patrimony quickly in travel and gambling, and was forced to earn his living by journalism, contributing to *Punch* and Fraser's Magazine and editing *Cornhill*, though he could also have been a graphic artist. His great work is *Vanity Fair* (1848). He died in 1863.

Edward Thomas was born in London in 1878 and married while still an undergraduate at Lincoln College, Oxford. He supported his wife Helen Noble as best he could by hack writing and did not take his poetry too seriously until advised of its excellence by Robert Frost. He died in action at Arras in 1917.

Francis Thompson was born in Preston, Lancashire, in 1859 and educated for the priesthood at Ushaw College near Durham. Finding that he had no vocation, he tried medicine in Manchester but did not graduate and ended an opium addict on the streets of London. He was rescued from this plight by the poet Alice Meynell and her husband who arranged for convalescence at Storrington Priory in Sussex where he wrote some memorable religious poetry. He was tended for the rest of his life by the Meynells, dying of chronic tuberculosis in 1907.

Edmund Waller was born near Amersham in Hertfordshire in 1606 and educated at Eton and King's College, Cambridge. He represented various constituencies and was a member of the Long Parliament from 1640 until 1643, when his complicity in 'Waller's Plot', a Royalist conspiracy, caused him to be arrested and expelled. He avoided execution by abject confession, the payment of large fine and acceptance of exile. The banishment was revoked in 1651 and he proved himself equally apt at praising the Lord Protector and the returned Charles II, writing *To the King upon his Majesty's Happy Return* in 1660. He died in 1687.

Robert Wever (fl. 1550) was a sixteenth-century dramatist now known mainly for the lyric 'In Youth Is Pleasure'.

William Wordsworth was born in Cockermouth, Cumberland in 1770, the son of a lawyer who died when he was sixteen. He was educated at St John's College Cambridge and during a sojourn in France experienced the excitement of the early revolution ('Bliss was it in that dawn . . .'). He had an affair with Annette Vallon, the daughter of a Blois surgeon. She bore his child Ann Caroline, whom he acknowledged at the christening. He did not marry the mother, and the Terror and declaration of war by England in 1793 drove him home. He gradually lost his republicanism but his life thereafter was plagued by recurring guilt. While living with his sister Dorothy in Somerset he became friendly with Coleridge, with whom he published the *Lyrical Ballads* (1798). The preface to this collection denied the need for stylised language or elaborate conceits in poetry. In 1800 he went with Dorothy to live at Grasmere in the Lake District and married his cousin, Mary Hutchinson, two years later. He became Poet Laureate in 1843 on the death of Robert Southey and died in 1850, having lived comfortably on sinecures and state pensions for the last fifty years of his life.